Kokoro no Te
Handmade Treasures from the Heart

Kumiko Sudo

Breckling Press

Library of Congress Cataloging-in-Publication Data

Sudo, Kumiko.

　Kokoro no te : handmade treasures from the heart / Kumiko Sudo.

　　　p. cm.

　　ISBN 1-933308-04-4

　　1. Textile crafts—Japan.　2. Fancy work—Japan.　3. Gifts—Japan.

　I. Title: Handmade treasures from the heart.　II. Title.

　　TT699.S835 2005

　　746—dc22   2005020608

This book was set in Bembo and Cronos Pro by Bartko Design, Inc.

Editorial direction by Anne Knudsen

Cover and interior design by Kim Bartko

Cover and interior photographs by Sharon Hoogstraten

Calligraphy and water color paintings by Kumiko Sudo

Technical drawings by Kandy Petersen

With special thanks to Yuwa Fabric Company and National Nonwovens for their support.

Published by Breckling Press

283 N. Michigan Ave., Elmhurst, IL 60126

Printed and bound in China

International Standard Book Number: 1-933308-04-4

Contents

Kokoro no Te is a celebration of the glory of nature.
Handmade from the heart, these simple treasures
are my way of sharing my impressions of
natural beauty with you.

Preface

TRANSLATED FROM THE JAPANESE, *Kokoro* means heart. Just as in the English language, this word has many connotations. *Kokoro* can mean friendship, generosity of spirit, or loving kindness. It is the living center of a family, a village, even the world. Combined with the Japanese word *Te*, which translates as hand, a beautiful meaning becomes clear. When a gift is made by hand and given with the heart, good wishes and good fortune are extended from one person to another in loving harmony.

The creations in *Kokoro no Te* are my way of offering a loving heart to the world around me. My inspiration and my happiness come from nature. Each day in small ways I celebrate the joys of creation—the fragrance of lilacs floating in a breeze, dewdrops on a morning glory, the rustle of grasses, and the little feet of birds as they hop across fallen leaves. As sensations like these melt deep into my heart, my hands become busy. I choose fabrics and threads, and my mind's eye molds them into shapes anew. I quietly stitch and soon I have made a little treasure that delicately reflects the beauty of flower or bud or the free spirit of the tiny creature that inspired it. When I give this treasure as a gift, I am presenting a piece of my heart, extending friendship and sharing happiness.

Kumiko Sudo

A Guide to Technique

In *Kokoro no Te* you will find thirty
small projects, designed to be made
by hand and given as gifts that come
straight from the heart. You will
quickly see that many of the projects
incorporate materials and techniques
that I have not shared in my previous
books. Here, for instance, I invite you
to rediscover felt, a fabric most of
us enjoyed working with as children
because of the ease with which it can
be sewn. Several projects include

beading and embroidery. I encourage you to find joy in adding your own embellishments to each project, making each gift you give unique. Some of the projects are very simple and can be completed in less than an hour. *Persimmon Pincushion*, *Windmill*, and, of course, my fabric thimbles are all easy to make. Other projects, such as *Evening Elegance* or the Japanese *Temari* handballs, take a little more time and patience, yet these are the one that will give you the most pleasure.

Fabrics

The projects in *Kokoro no Te* present you with a wonderful opportunity to showcase special fabrics. Many of the samples photographed are crafted from Japanese silks, *shiboris* or *chiromen* crepe; other are made from beautifully designed and readily available contemporary cottons. For years, I have collected traditional Japanese textiles, and I now have a large selection of antique kimono and obi. I have cut up several of them in order to incorporate their rich colors and patterns into my designs. I save each scrap, no matter how small, to make small gifts like the ones in this book.

To make the designs in *Kokoro no Te*, you do not need to have a large fabric collection, nor do you need to spend a lot of money. The projects are intended to be made from small scraps and you can easily mix and match fabrics within a single design. For this reason, I have not specified yardages for any of the projects. Even for some of the larger purses, you will need no more than a sixteenth of a yard of any particular fabric. If you are shopping for new fabrics, I suggest you buy ⅛ yard of every fabric that catches your eye and ¼ yard of those that are irresistible. This way, you will

Sewing Kit

Kokoro no Te is designed as a collection of take-along projects, requiring only basic sewing tools that will fit easily into a small tote. A materials list is supplied with each project. In addition, keep the following items close to hand.

Hand-sewing needles	Quality threads in variety of colors	Eraser
Embroidery needles (large eye)	Cotton stuffing or batting scraps	Tailor's chalk or non-
Pins and pincushion	Thread snips	permanent marker
Thimble	Fabric scissors	Ruler
Quality embroidery floss in	Paper scissors	Flexible tape measure
variety of colors	Sharp pencils	Toothpick or dollmaker's awl

have enough fabric for two, three, or more of the project you are making. Look for a variety of colors and shades, and try to find some fabrics with strong motifs that you will be able to highlight in a pleasing way. Using the photographs as a guide to contrast, I suggest you select colors and patterns that you enjoy the most. It is the combinations you choose that will make your gifts unique.

Working with Felts

Several of the projects in *Kokoro no Te* incorporate felt. Soft to the touch, I particularly like to use felt as the lining for purses and pouches. You can slip jewelry or special keepsakes inside, knowing that the felt lining will keep them safe and scratch-free. Quality felts are available by the yard from several companies. I particularly like the all-natural wool felts from National Nonwovens. They come in rich textures and a variety of luxurious colors. Avoid pre-cut craft felts,

which are usually rough to the touch and may bleed upon exposure to damp.

Quality felt is a delight to sew. Since it doesn't fray, there is no need for hemming. It holds even the smallest stitches securely. Use matching-color thread and your stitches will sink into the felt and become invisible. For several of the small pouches and totes in *Kokoro no Te*, I slip pieces of felt inside the outer fabric, giving the project a soft, padded feel.

Cutting

Full-size templates are provided for all pieces other than simple squares, circles, and rectangles. Read the pattern and the template pieces carefully to make sure you allow the correct seam allowance for each piece. Most purse pieces, for instance, require a generous ½″ seam allowance, while templates for smaller projects use ¼″ or even ⅛″ seam allowances. For squares and rectangles, the seam allowance is already included in the measurement provided. Felt, used as lining for most of the projects, requires no seam allowance at all. Since the templates are all quite small and multiples of the same piece are rarely needed, I use sharp scissors rather than rotary cutting equipment. Whichever method you use, remember to transfer any markings from the pattern onto the cut pieces of fabric.

Sewing

I sew everything—straight seams and curved seams, piecing and appliqué—by hand. When I sew, I feel my hands are directed by my heart, and I like the sense of intimacy that hand-sewing gives me. I am particularly sensitive to this emotion when I am making gifts. Since all the projects in *Kokoro no Te* are quite small, you may want to sew them by hand, too. If you prefer to sew by machine, you will find that straight seams, such as the side seams in most of the purse projects, turn out beautifully. In certain projects, however, where you may need to manipulate the fabric as you sew, you may find that hand-sewing is not only faster, but more accurate.

Many of the designs involve sewing curved seams. For perfect curved seams, I use a form of appliqué or invisible stitching that is described below. My technique involves placing a fabric piece, with the seam allowance folded under, on top of a background piece; the piece is then blind-stitched by hand. In the instructions, this is what is meant by the term *appliqué*. The term *sew* indicates a more traditional method of sewing the pieces together, right sides facing, using a running stitch along the seam lines. Straight seams are sewn in this way, and you may use hand or machine stitching.

Coil Stitch

For some of the projects in *Kokoro no Te*, I have used a form of overstitch named *coil stitch*. It is helpful when joining the edges of two pieces together. For instance, when making the felt "pincushion" that wraps around one the hearts in *Ivy Pocket* on page 79, coil stitch allows you to butt the front and side pieces up against each other and sew neatly, evenly, and

Coil stitch—begin with backstitches, work from right to left, end with backstitches

without puckers around the heart-shaped edge. The bottom of *Heian Pin-Pin* on page 85 is also attached using coil stitch.

Pin two pieces right sides together, aligning the edges. Knot the thread and begin with a double backstitch. Taking one stitch at a time and working from right to left, insert the needle at a 45° angle through the front fabric facing you. Push through all layers and exit the needle at the back of the work, ⅛" or less to the left of your entry point. Tug the thread then loop over the top of the work to take your next stitch. When you reach the end of your row of stitches, take three backstitches to secure. Turn the work right side out. The line of stitches on the back of your work will be on the diagonal; the stitches at the front will be near-invisible and recessed into the fabric.

Fabric Origami

Many of the projects in *Kokoro no Te* incorporate fabric origami, or the folding of fabric to create new shapes. The flowers that embellish *Bird of Paradise* on page 17 and *Camellia Cozy* on page 27 are folded from simple shapes. Even if you know nothing of traditional Japanese origami (paper folding), you will find that my fabric-folding techniques are easy to learn. These tips may help.

- A key difference between folding paper and folding fabric is that paper is available with different colors on the two sides. To achieve the same effect with fabric, you must first sew the two colors of your choice together, then turn them right side out and press. Often, finger pressing will be adequate. Directions for this step are provided with each pattern.

- Study each folding diagram carefully before you begin. Determine which is the right and wrong side of the fabric. Go through the step-by-step instructions mentally before you even pick up the fabric. You may find it helpful to practice each new shape on a sample so that you solve any difficulties before you begin your final piece.
- Always fold accurately and neatly.
- Crease each fold firmly with the back of your thumbnail. Good creases make the folding easier, and they serve as guides to future steps.

You will find that the same procedures are used over and over again. You will soon become so proficient with them that you can carry them out almost without thinking.

Beading

I have always loved beads and enjoy incorporating them into my sewing. Almost all of the projects in *Kokoro no Te* are embellished with beads. Beading is simple and does not take much time or practice, yet it lends a wonderful new dimension to fashion accessories, purses, or decorative accents.

Types of Beads

Today, there is an incredible variety of beads available from specialty bead stores, catalogs, and web sites. Crafts stores

also carry beautiful selections. Because the projects in *Kokoro no Te* are small scale, I tend to choose small beads. I particularly enjoy highlighting the beautiful patterns I find in fabric with delicate placement of seed beads. My favorites are Japanese Delica (size 11—the larger the size number, the smaller the bead), which are tiny cylinders, no more than 2 mm long. They come is an amazing variety of colors and finishes. Delicas are easy to sew, lying flat against the fabric and adding texture, dimension, and shine. *Bird of Paradise* on page 17, *Kara Lily Caddy* on page 43, and *Acorn* on page 61 are just a few of the projects that feature Delicas. I sometimes use Czech seed beads, which have a more rounded shape, in place of Delicas. I also like longer cylinder beads, such as 3 mm Delicas (size 8). Notice how this selection draws attention the subtle design on the fabric on the back of *Bird of Paradise*. Bugle beads are another favorite. These longer cylinders come in a variety of lengths. *Fishie Pouch* on page 121 and *Cicada* on page 133 feature ¾″ bugles.

I use small round beads both for sewing directly onto projects, as in *Fishie Pouch,* and, more often, to string handles for purses. Depending on the scale of the project, they may measure anywhere from 3 mm to 6 mm. On occasion, I allow beads to be a focal point of a design and choose beautiful lampwork beads, like the one on *Tomato Cache* on page 23 or other elaborate varieties, as on *Evening Elegance* on page 35. It is fun to spend an hour or two in a specialty store to find beads that will be perfect for your sewing projects.

Sewing Beads

While there are specialty threads available from bead stores, designed for sewing beads, I tend to use a strong, high-quality hand-sewing thread. I use a simple running stitch to sew seed beads or small round beads in place. Sometimes, I follow the design in the fabric or follow the shape of a particular template; other times I place beads to reflect the veins of a leaf, as in *Brilliance* on page 57 or *Mallow Rose* on page 93. My technique is always the same—a simple running stitch that neatly hides the thread.

I secure larger beads by stitching through them two or three times. Sometimes it is necessary to "lock" beads in place, using a small bead or seed bead. I simply stack the desired beads, then run the thread through them as shown. The tiny bead on top locks the others in place, as in *Tidy Tote* on page 75. The thread goes through the first and second beads, then through one side of the seed bead and out the other, and back down into the other two beads.

Stringing beads for purse hands is easy and fun. Knot a strand of two-ply embroidery floss or beading thread. Make a stitch to secure it at the spot where the handle starts. String beads in the desired pattern, then make a double stitch at the point where the handle ends.

Embroidery

Adding embroidery is a simple and delicate way to bring subtle highlights to your sewing projects. For the projects in *Kokoro no Te*, there is no need to master a variety of stitches. A few key skills that require minimal practice are all you need.

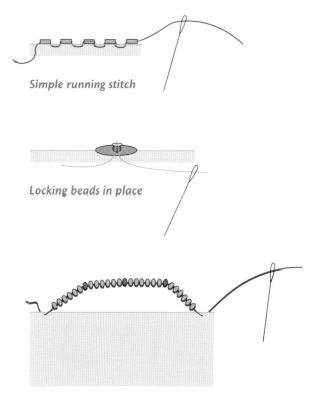

Simple running stitch

Locking beads in place

String beads for purse handle

Herringbone Stitch

I use two-ply embroidery floss and a simple herringbone stitch to sew together the fronts and backs of all the purses and pouches in *Kokoro no Te*. Pin the front and back together, aligning any curves. Hide the knot on the inside of the purse, on the bottom layer of fabric, exiting the needle at the front. Draw the thread upwards and diagonally to the right, then make a small stitch into the top layer of fabric. The needle exits immediately to the left of its entry point. Draw the thread downwards and diagonally to the right, then make a tiny stitch in the bottom layer of fabric, again exiting the needle immediately to the left of its entry point. Continue to the end, then make a double stitch to secure.

Stem Stitch

For *Apple Pocket* on page 47 and *Brilliance* on page 57, I used stem stitch to embroider a pattern of leaf veins. It is easy to work freehand or, if you need a guideline, mark the pattern with tailor's chalk. Stem stitch is simply a line of staggered backstitches, each about ⅛″ long or less. Hide the knot on the underside of the fabric. Draw the thread through the fabric and re-enter about ⅛″ or desired stitch length along your marked pattern. Turn the needle and come up again about half-way along and closely next to the first stitch. Take another stitch, progressing about ⅛″ along your pattern. Repeat and continue to the end.

Herringbone stitch

Stem stitch

Embroidered Chain or Braid

Apple Pocket on page 47 features pretty little buds that dangle
elegantly from short embroidered chains. If you wish, you
can add buds like these to any of the projects in *Kokoro no Te*
or to designs of your own creation. Choose three-ply
embroidery thread. Hide the knot at the underside edge
of the purse, exactly where you want the chain to begin,
exiting the needle at the front edge. Make a small stitch to
secure, leaving a small loop (⅛″ or less) of thread. Holding
the thread to the right, enter the needle from the back of
the loop to the front, leaving another small loop. Repeat
until chain is desired length. Make a stitch to attach bud.

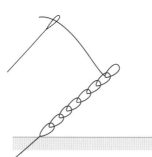

Embroidered chain

"Just as there is a key to every locked door, there are special ways to open the creative mind. On a sunrise walk, the dewdrops on a wakening leaf catch my eye. On the underside of the leaf, 1 spy a snail who has finished his breakfast and is inching back into the cool grass, leaving a trail behind him. A morning glory rouses with a yawn, stretching out its delicate petals. 1 raise my eyes to the skyline, where, little by little, pinks and lavenders give way to morning blue. Whirls of morning mist mix the ever-changing hues. A profusion of colors and patterns rushes into my mind. The lock turns and the door is open."

Purses, Totes, and Keepsakes

SCRAPS OF BEAUTIFULLY designed silks, often left over from custom-tailored kimono or obi, were traditionally used to create Japanese "tea crafts"— small, treasured items like the elegant purses and pouches shown here. Imagine a hand-held cache designed to match a young girl's first kimono. Today, concoctions like these make an instant fashion statement— irresistibly elegant.

Bird of Paradise

This sweet confection presents a delightful opportunity to use exquisite pieces of decorative fabric. Let the fabric guide you in your choice of beads, and position them to highlight the fabric design. Three pretty flower petals and the beautiful center beads combine to suggest a bird in flight.

See templates on pages 136–137. Use ½" seam allowance for purse pieces only; use ¼" seam allowance for other sewing.

Purse

1. With template A, cut three from felt. Add ½" seam allowance, then cut one from fabric for purse back. With templates B and C, cut one each from felt. Adding ½" seam allowance, cut one each for purse front. Fold in seam allowances on each fabric piece and press to hold. Slip a felt piece inside folded-in seam allowance of its corresponding fabric piece. Sew felt to folded-in seam allowance, taking care not to let needle go through to

SELECTIONS

Purse fabric: cotton or silk with suggestive motifs or summertime patterns

Lining: felt in contrast color

Flowers: two contrasting fabrics—colorful, patterned fabric for outside and subtle colors for inside

Beads: large decorative centerpiece bead (about ⅝"), locked in place with small round bead (⅛"); about 130 seed beads for front; if desired, about 20 small tubular beads to highlight portions of fabric design on purse back

Embroidery floss

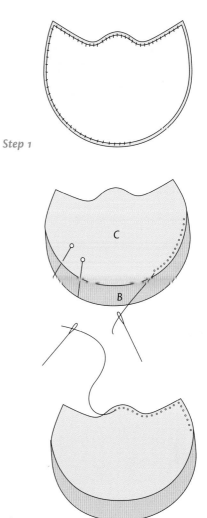

Step 1

purse front. If desired, add small beads to highlight design on purse back.

2. Position felt-backed piece C to overlap felt-backed piece B, aligning so that C/B is exactly same size and shape as A. Pin and baste along curve. Use small running stitches to sew B to C, locking a seed bead in place with every stitch, thus disguising stitches on purse front. Do this along curve only, leaving top and top 2″ of sides unbeaded. Remove any basting stitches. Use small running stitches to sew remaining beads to felt-backed C.

3. Using a tiny overstitch, sew remaining two felt A pieces to back and front of purse, forming lining.

4. Wrong sides together and leaving top 2″ along each side open, sew around rest of curve using embroidery floss and herringbone stitch (see page 12).

Step 2

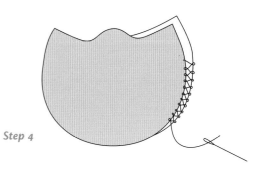

Step 4

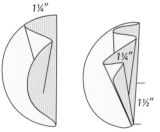

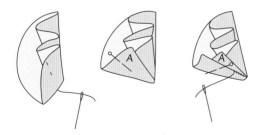

Step 6

Flower

5. Using combination of plain and patterned fabrics, cut six circles measuring 4½″ in diameter (this includes ¼″ seam allowance). Pairing a patterned circle to a plainer circle and right sides together, sew together around circumference, leaving about 1″ open. Turn right side out, press, then blind stitch opening closed. Press lightly to reinforce shape.

6. Fold in half, then make folds as shown, beginning about 1¼″ from center top. Pin or press to hold. From back, make about four stitches through folds to hold in place. Bring

thread to back, without cutting. Fold or squeeze point A inwards, forming flower tip. Pin. Using same thread, make three or four stitches to hold.

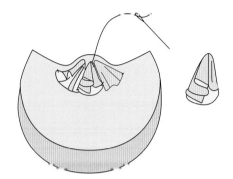

Step 7

Complete

7. When all three flower petals are complete, stitch tip of each securely to purse front. Make additional stitches at far left and far right as shown. If desired, make final stitches attaching petals together.

8. Sew decorative bead in position, locking in place with smaller bead.

Tomato Cache

A pretty jewelry case or a cache for a special gift, Tomato Cache *beautifully combines fabric, felt, silk ribbon, and beads. Carry it with you or pin it to the wall of your sewing room or office to keep favorite items safe.*

See templates on pages 138–139. Use ½" seam allowance for purse pieces only; use ¼" seam allowance for other sewing.

Buds

1. Cut eight circles measuring 1¾" from a wide silk ribbon or from silk. Fold in half, then fold inwards from either side as shown. Gather stitch along top, then pull gathers gently to create flower shape. Stitch to hold. Make eight.

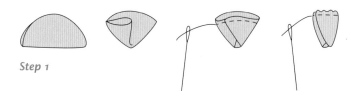

Step 1

SELECTIONS

Purse fabric: cotton or silk

Lining: felt in contrast colors

Buds: silk scraps or silk ribbon

Beads: one large, two medium, and three small for centerpiece; about 100 colorful seed beads for felt leaf; if desired, about 50 seed beads to highlight portions of fabric design

Embroidery floss

2. With template A, cut four from felt. Add ½″ seam allowance, then cut one from fabric for purse back. With template B and adding ½″ seam allowance, cut one from fabric for bottom front. With template C, cut one from felt for top front. Fold in seam allowances on each fabric piece and press to hold. Slip a corresponding felt piece inside folded-in seam allowance of fabric pieces A and B. Sew felt to folded-in seam allowance, taking care not to let needle go through to purse front. If desired, highlight a portion of design on purse back by adding a subtle pattern of beads. Sew one of remaining felt A pieces to felt-backed B piece.

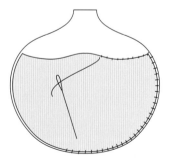

Step 2

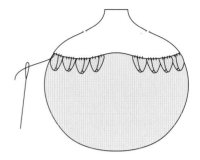

Step 3

3. Sew eight flower pieces in place as shown onto purse front.

4. Position leaf piece C on purse front, slightly overlapping B and hiding top edges of flowers. Pin and baste to hold. Use small running stitches to sew C in position, locking a seed bead in place with every stitch, thus disguising stitches on purse front. Remove any basting stitches. String then sew one large, two medium, and six small decorative beads in place as shown.

Complete

5. Using a tiny overstitch, sew remaining two felt A pieces to back and front of purse, forming lining.

6. Wrong sides together and leaving leaf portion at top of design open, sew around entire curve using embroidery floss and herringbone stitch (see page 12).

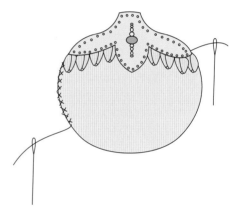

Step 4 and Step 6

Camellia Cozy

Tuck away your sunglasses or cell phone in this charming flower cozy. The soft felt interior will keep them safe and scratch-free. If you wish, add a ribbon loop at the back and keep the cozy on a hook near the door so that you can always find your sunglasses or phone when you need them!

See templates on page 140. Use ½" seam allowance for purse pieces only; use ¼" seam allowance for other sewing.

Cozy

1. With template A, cut four from felt. Add ½" seam allowance then cut two more from fabric. Fold in seam allowances on fabric pieces and press to hold. Slip a felt piece inside folded-in seam allowance of each fabric piece. Sew felt to folded-in seam allowance, taking care not to let needle go through to purse front. Sew large beads to front and back as desired.

2. Cut two strips of felt measuring 1½" × 7½" for stems. Roll one side to center vertically and overstitch in place. Roll other side over previously rolled section and stitch.

SELECTIONS

Cozy fabric: cotton or silk

Lining: felt in contrast color

Flower: silk or cotton scrap; felt scraps in three colors plus two shades of green for leaves; felt scraps for stems

Beads: four large beads for embellishing cozy; sixteen small beads for flower centers; about 150 seed beads for leaves

Embroidery floss

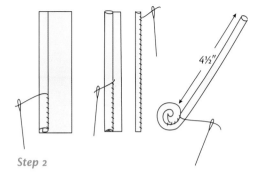

Step 2

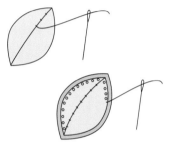

Step 3

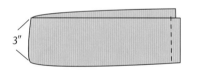

3″

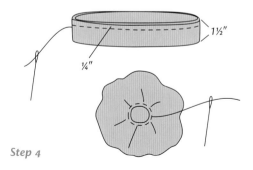

1½″

¼″

Step 4

4½″

Curl at one end to form a swirl, leaving about 4½″ uncurled. Overstitch curl to hold.

Flower

3. With templates B and C, cut three each from two different shades of green felt. Embroider a delicate leaf-vein pattern that curves across center of each C piece (see stem stitch on page 12). Position C on top of B and pin to hold. Sew B to C, locking tiny beads in place as you sew. Make three.

4. Cut strip of fabric measuring 3″ × 12″. Sew ends together to make loop. Fold in half horizontally to make 1½″ wide loop. Gather stitch along unfolded side, pull gathers to form flower shape, then backstitch to hold.

5. Cut three circles from brightly colored felts, measuring 1¼″, 1″, and ⅝″ in diameter. Repeat to cut a second set. Stack

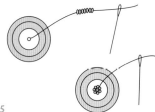

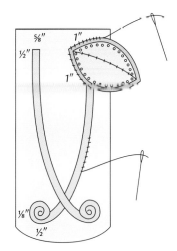

each set from largest to smallest, then sew a single bead at center, stitching through all layers. String then stitch 7 more beads around center bead.

6. Sew stems securely in place on cozy front. Position two leaves, overlapping tops of stems. Stitch just enough to hold in place. Stitch securely around circumference of middle circle, going through all layers, to hold flower in place. Sew remaining leaf and flower center to back of cozy.

Complete

7. Using a tiny overstitch, sew remaining two felt A pieces to back and front of cozy, forming lining. Wrong sides together and leaving about 1½″ open at top of each side, sew back and front together using embroidery floss and herringbone stitch (see page 12).

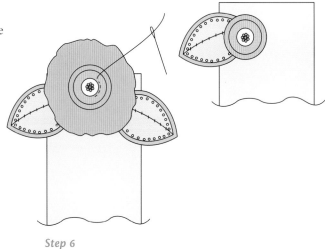

Step 6

Posy Wristlet

Sweet and simple, Posy Wristlet is a lovely accessory for prom night. Or pop candies inside and arrange around the table as hand-made tokens at wedding or baby showers.

See template on pages 141. Use ¼" seam allowance unless otherwise indicated.

Wristlet

1. Using template A, cut five each from two complementary fabrics. Sew same-fabric pieces together along sides as shown, making outer ring and inner petals. Position right sides together, then use running stitch to sew along outer edge. Turn right side out. Press.

2. For inner pouch, cut two with template B. Wrong sides together, sew diagonal sides, then turn right side out. Position inside petal ring, with reverse side of petal ring showing. Sew in place around top. Push pouch through petal

SELECTIONS

Fabrics: combination of soft shades or pastels for inner pouch, outer pouch, and drawstring buds

Decorative drawstring: about 30" long

Step 1

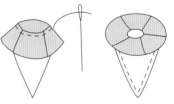

Step 2

Step 3

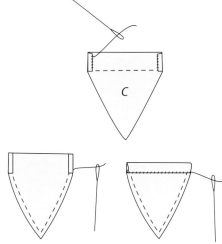

Step 4

ring, so that front of petal ring and wrong side of pouch now show.

3. Run pretty rows of stitches along seam lines between individual petal pieces, making seams more pronounced.

4. For outer pouch, cut two with template C. Mark fold line on fabric. On each piece, roll or fold side edges inwards three times, securing with overstitches as shown. Position two C pieces right sides together. Sew diagonal sides as shown, taking care not to stitch into fold-overs. Turn over raw edge at top, then fold as shown and overstitch in place, creating drawstring tube. Turn right side out.

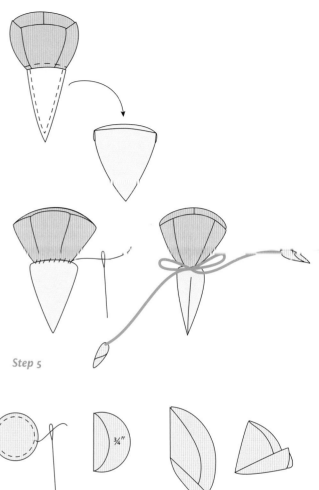

5. Insert inner pouch into outer pouch and overstitch in place. Feed drawstring through tube. Knot each end.

Step 5

Drawstring Buds

6. Cut two fabric circles, measuring 3″ in diameter. Turn in raw edge by ¼″, press, then stitch in place. Fold then roll fabric as shown. Stitch loose edge in place. Gather stitch around wide end. Insert knotted drawstring, then pull gathers and backstitch to hold. Make two.

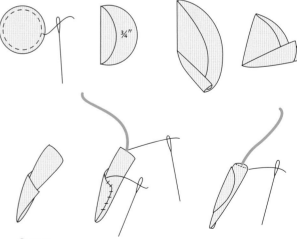

Step 6

Evening Elegance

This sensational take-along clutch prettily accommodates evening essentials while making a unique fashion statement. Beautiful fabrics, ribbons and beads—make it as a gift that will be treasured and remembered. I was fortunate to find a single piece of fabric with the perfect design for the purse back. You can recreate this look by choosing two complimentary fabrics, backing each in felt, then sewing them together along the bead line. Bird of Paradise *on page 17 is made this way.*

See templates on pages 142–143. Use ½" seam allowance for purse pieces only; use ¼" seam allowance for other sewing.

Buds

1. See *Tomato Cache* on page 23 to make five buds. Fold 2" strips of ¼" silk ribbon as shown to makes leaves. Press. Sew to buds.

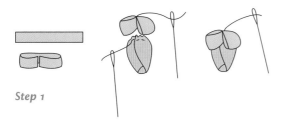

Step 1

SELECTIONS

Purse fabric: three complementary cottons or silks; felt for top front

Lining: felt in contrast color

Buds: silk or silk ribbon; ¼" silk ribbon for leaves

Beads: two large decorative beads for centerpiece; about 150 seed beads for front and back

Embroidery floss

Clutch

1. With template A, cut four from felt. Add ½″ seam allowance, then cut one each from two different fabrics. With template B and adding ½″ seam allowance, cut one from fabric. Fold in seam allowances of each fabric piece and press to hold. Position then pin or baste fabric piece B so that it very slightly overlaps fabric piece A (front). Using tiny overstitch, carefully sew around curve at center front of purse, joining B to A. Trim away excess fabric beneath B piece. Slip

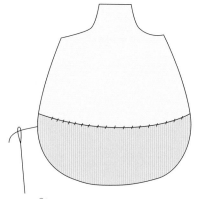

Step 1

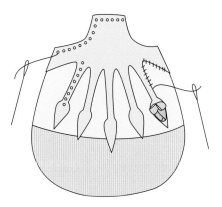

Step 4

a felt piece inside folded-in seam allowances of this combined A/B piece and inside remaining fabric A piece. Sew together, sewing felt to folded-in seam allowance, taking care not to let needle go through to purse front. Add small beads as desired to highlight design on purse front and back.

4. Use template C to carefully cut leaf shape from felt. Sew seed beads, buds, and ribbons in position as in photograph. Position C on purse front, with tips slightly overlapping B. Pin and baste to hold. Use small running stitches to sew C. Remove any basting stitches. Position then sew large decorative beads in place.

Complete

5. Using a tiny overstitch, sew remaining two felt A pieces to back and front of purse, forming lining.

6. Wrong sides together and leaving top 2″ along each side open, sew around rest of curve using embroidery floss and herringbone stitch (see page 12).

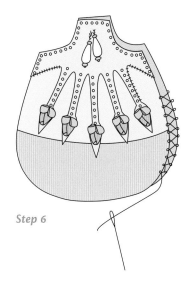

Step 6

Wisteria Pouch

A pretty fashion accessory, Wisteria Pouch *can be held by its drawstrings or wrapped around the wrist. Simpler still, tuck a favorite keepsake inside or fill it with candies for Valentine's Day.*

Use ¼" seam allowance unless otherwise indicated.

Petals

1. Cut 17 circles measuring 3" diameter. Fold in half, right side out, then fold inwards along fold-lines shown. Gather stitch around curve through all layers. For all but two petals, pull gathers gently, until petal top measures about ¾", then backstitch to hold. Leave needle in remaining two petals.

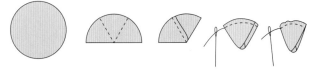

Step 1

Pouch: complementary cottons or silks for purse and
    drawstring tube

Lining: cotton or silk in contrast color

Flowers: selection of multi-colored decorative fabrics

Drawstrings: two 30" decorative drawstrings

Plain shirt button

Batting scrap

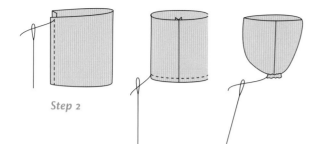

Step 2

Step 3

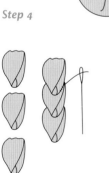

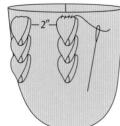

Step 4

Step 5

Pouch

2. Cut strips of fabric measuring 5″ × 10″—one for outer pouch and other for lining. Fold in half lengthwise and stitch seam. Set lining aside. Turn outer pouch right side out and gather stitch along bottom edge. Pull thread tightly to gather and backstitch to hold. Fold top edge inwards by ¼″ and press or baste to hold.

3. Turn lining piece wrong side out, then fold A to B to meet at center and make single stitch to hold. Sew four short seams as shown. Do not turn right side out. Fold top edge of lining inwards by ¼″ and press or baste to hold. Set aside.

4. Cut a 1⅜″ circle from lining fabric. Fold in row edges and press to hold. Gather stitch around circumference but do not cut thread. Place a small piece of batting or stuffing at center, with a small shirt button on top. Pull gathers tight, backstitch to hold, then sew to outside bottom of outer pouch.

5. Sew buds together in five sets of three as shown. Sew each set to pouch, leaving about 2″ between each set.

6. Cut two strips measuring 1½″ × 6″ for drawstring tubes. Fold edges in by ¼″ three times, Stitch in place. Fold in half lengthwise and press. Right sides together, stitch first strip to outer pouch. Add second strip, taking care not to overlap edges. Fold each strip to inside and blind stitch in place, creating drawstring tube.

7. Insert lining into outer pouch. Overstitch turned-in seam allowance at top of lining to base of drawstring tube. Feed two drawstrings through tube. Knot ends. Slip one knot into each of partially made petals from Step 1. Pull gathers tight, trapping knot, and backstitch to hold.

8. Cut two fabric circles, measuring 1″ in diameter. Turn under raw edges, then gather stitch. Add batting or stuffing and position knot of drawstring at center. Trap knot and batting by pulling gathers tight. Backstitch to hold. Make two.

Step 6

Step 7

Step 8

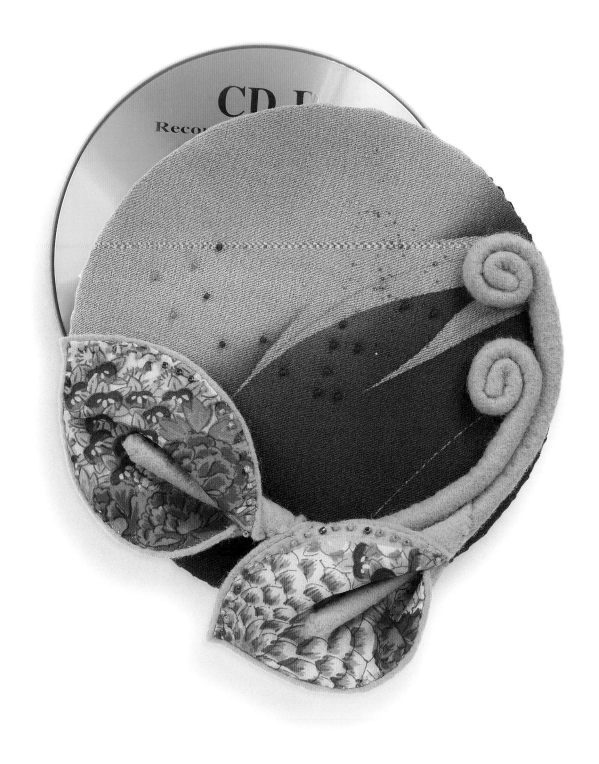

Kara Lily Caddy

A stunning fashion accessory, **Kara Lily Caddy** *also makes a unique gift-wrap—imagine opening up the pouch to find a CD with family photos tucked inside!*

See template on page 144. Use ¼" seam allowance unless otherwise indicated.

Caddy

1. Cut four circles measuring 5½" from felt. Cut two circles measuring 6½" from fabric. Fold in ½" seam allowances on fabric pieces and press to hold. Slip a felt piece inside folded-in seam allowance of each fabric piece. Sew felt to folded-in seam allowance, taking care not to let needle go through to purse front. As desired, sew seed beads to highlight portions of design on back and front.

SELECTIONS

Fabric: cotton or silk

Lining: felt in contrast color

Flower: silk or cotton scraps; felt scraps

Beads: about 70 seed beads

Embroidery floss

Step 4

2. Using a tiny overstitch, sew remaining two felt A pieces to back and front of purse, forming lining.

3. Cut two strips of felt measuring 1½″ × 7″ for stems. Follow Step 2 of *Camellia Cozy* on page 27 to make stems, leaving about 5″ uncurled.

Flower

4. With template A, cut two from felt and two from fabric. Fold in raw edges of fabric piece by about ⅛″ and use a tiny overstitch to sew it in place on top of felt piece. Make two.

5. Wrap leaves around stems, about 2″ from stem top, and sew in place. Decorate front and back of flowers with seed beads as in photographs. Sew stems and flowers securely to purse front.

2″

3½″

2½″

Step 5

Complete

6. Wrong sides together and leaving portion without flower decoration open, sew back and front together using embroidery floss and herringbone stitch (see page 12).

Apple Pocket

Here is the prefect end-of-year gift for teacher—just pop a gift certificate or other small token inside. No teacher could possibly feel underappreciated!

See template on page 145. See templates on page oo. Use ½" seam allowance for purse pieces only; use ¼" seam allowance for other sewing.

Pocket

1. With template A, cut four from felt. Add ½" seam allowance, then cut two from fabric. Fold in seam allowances on fabric pieces and press to hold. Slip a felt piece inside folded-in seam allowance of each fabric piece. Sew felt to folded-in seam allowance, taking care not to let needle go through to purse front. As desired, sew seed beads to highlight portions of design on back and front.

2. With template B, cut one from felt. Embroider as desired then add beads as shown. For stem stitch embroidery, see page 12. Turn over, then fold and roll so that beads show all

SELECTIONS

Fabric: cotton or silk

Lining: felt in complementary color

Flower: felt scraps for leaves, silk scraps and silk
   ribbon for buds

Beads: about 75 seed beads

⅛" ribbon

Embroidery floss

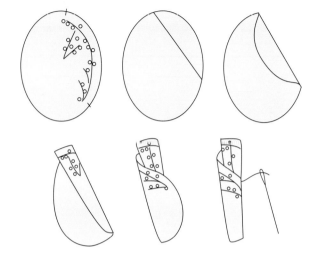

Step 2

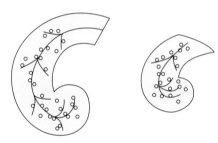

Step 3

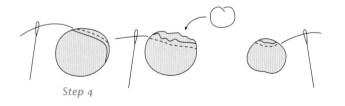

Step 4

around stem. Stitch to hold, then sew bottom edge in place to inside of pouch front, at top center.

3. With templates C and D, cut two each from felt. On one of each shape, embroider to imitate leaf veins and add beads as shown. Use tiny overstitch to sew C pieces together and D pieces together around outside edges. Stitch top edge of C to inside of purse front, as shown in photograph. Stitch D to purse front.

Buds

4. To make fabric buds, cut two circles measuring 2″ in diameter and three circles measuring 1½″. Gather stitch around circumference, then place batting or stuffing at center, and pull gathers tight. Backstitch to hold.

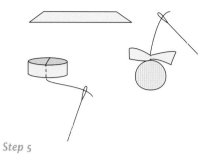

5. Cut five 2″ lengths of ¼″ ribbon. Fold in half from end to end, then stitch through both layers at center as shown. Stitch to top of each bud.

Step 5

6. Take a needle threaded with embroidery floss through top of bud, hiding knot. Use button-hole stitch to create braid (see page 13). Braid is about 1″ long for small buds and 2″ long for large buds. Attach end of braid to base of stem at purse front.

Complete

7. Using a tiny overstitch, sew remaining two felt A pieces to back and front of purse, forming lining and trapping stem, leaf, and embroidery threads in place.

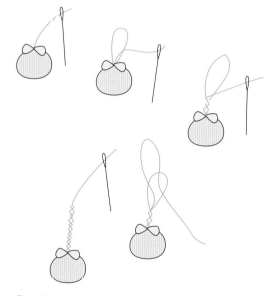

Step 6

"I constantly draw from nature to inspire me, and that is why I designed my sewing studio to look out into my gardens. Gazing through the glass doors, everything I see has the potential to transform into a motif or theme in my work. I see the velvet petals of a budding flower, the gentle wisps of white cloud in a summer sky, the busy buzzing of an industrious bee, or the playful tricks of squirrels or chipmunks as they dart across the pathways in my garden. My heart is overwhelmed with the joyful rhythms of nature and the ideas begin to flow."

Japan-Chic Fashion Pins

FEW ACCESSORIES are as simple or stunning as a decorative pin crafted from fabric and decorated with beads. These fabulous brooches are fun to make, and most are completed in less than an hour. Use them to add a splash of color and to dress up otherwise ordinary clothing and accessories. Or pin one to the top of a wrapped package as an extra special gift tag.

Honeysuckle

Simple to make, Honeysuckle *is a stunning accessory to a simple evening dress or jacket. The design beautifully melds fabric, silk ribbon, and felt.* Honeysuckle *comes together surprisingly quickly and is sure to win praise!*

See template on page 144. Use ¼" seam allowance for sewing.

Pin

1. Cut three circles from fabric, measuring 6" in diameter. Fold in half, right side out. Fold both sides inwards by 1½" and pin to hold. Gather stitch first circle along curved edge as shown and pull gathers gently; do not break thread. In same way, fold, pin, then gather next circle, using same thread. Repeat with third circle. Pull thread gently, creating

Step 1

1½"

SELECTIONS

Pin: cotton, silk, or rayon; felt in contrast color

Buds: 1" wired silk ribbon

Beads: about 20 seed beads

Cotton stuffing or batting scraps

Sew-on safety clasp

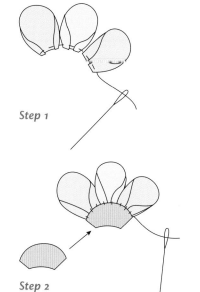

Step 1

Step 2

a semi-circle measuring about 2″. Pin to hold, but do not backstitch or cut thread yet.

2. With template A, cut two from felt for flower calyx. Sew one to each side of semi-circles from Step 1, easing gathers as necessary and trapping flower between felt pieces. Backstitch to secure gathers. Leave bottom of calyx open for stem.

3. Cut two strips of felt measuring 1½″ × 4½″ for stems. Follow Step 2 of *Camellia Cozy* on page 27 to make stems, leaving about 3½″ uncurled. Insert raw edge into calyx, then stitch opening closed. Stitch beads around semi-circle at pin front.

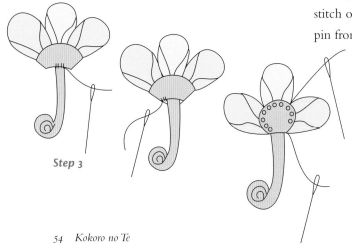

Step 3

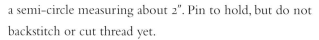

Honeysuckle *beautifully demonstrates how easy it is to blend different materials in the simplest of sewing projects. You can choose from silk, cotton, or rayon for the three leaves; the buds are made from wired silk ribbons; and the calyx and stem are crafted from soft felt. As an added embellishment, there are tiny seed beads sewn to the calyx. It's fun to shop for interesting beads or fabric, and it's even more enjoyable to sew with them.*

Step 4

Buds

4. Cut three lengths of wired silk ribbon, each measuring 1″ × 5″. Fold end to end, then stitch ends together to make loop. Gather stitch along one side, pull gathers, and backstitch to hold. Tuck batting or cotton inside, then gather stitch other side, pull gathers tight, and backstitch to hold.

5. Make braid measuring 1″ (see page 13). Sew to calyx, varying lengths of braids as desired. Make final stitch to attach curled end of stem to one of flowers.

6. Sew safety clasp to back of calyx.

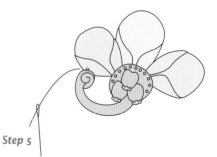

Step 5

Brilliance

Bold and colorful, Brilliance *demands attention. Designed as a keepsake pouch, it can also be worn as an oversize pocket or pin.*

See templates on page 146. Use ¼" seam allowance unless otherwise indicated.

Pin/Pouch

1. With template A, cut one from felt. Add ⅛" seam allowance around top curve only then cut one from fabric. Fold in seam around top curve by about ¼", then pin fabric piece on top of felt piece. About ⅛" of felt should show around curve. Overstitch around curve then use running stitch to sew raw edge of rest of fabric piece to felt.

2. Cut two B pieces from felt. Draw leaf-vein pattern onto one felt piece B. Embroider over lines, then add beads. (For stem stitch, see page 13.)

SELECTIONS

Pin/pouch: cotton or silk in two decorative patterns; felt in three colors

Yo-yos: scraps of silk or cotton

Artichoke flower: similar-color fabric and felt strips measuring 1¼" × 10"

Beads: about 150 seed beads

Embroidery floss

Sew-on safety clasp (optional)

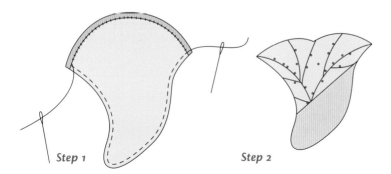

Step 1   *Step 2*

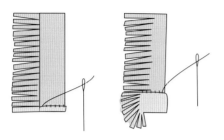

Step 4

Step 5

3. With template C, cut one from fabric adding ¼″ seam allowance. Fold in seam allowance and sew in place on top of B. Sew beads to top curve of B. Position this B/C piece on top of remaining felt B piece. Sew in place, adding beads around perimeter as you go.

Artichoke Flower

4. Make 1″ clips along one long side of fabric and felt strips. Place felt piece on top of fabric piece, then start rolling from one end to other. Make a row of stitches every so often to hold in place. Roll to end, then stitch to secure.

5. Cut strip of felt measuring 1½″ × 7″ for stem. Follow Step 2 of *Camellia Cozy* on page 27 to make stems, leaving about 4″ uncurled.

6. To make yo-yos, cut five circles of fabric measuring 3¼″ in diameter. Fold in raw edge by about ⅛″ and press to hold. Gather stitch around circumference. Pull gathers tight and backstitch. Press lightly. Sew three yo-yos around artichoke flower to form calyx.

7. Insert stem into base of flower and stitch in place. Make a few stitches to secure calyx yo-yos to stem.

Complete

8. Pin then sew B/C piece to A piece then sew together along sides and bottom. Sew remaining two yo-yos to back, overlapping edge a little. To wear *Brilliance* as pin, add sew-on clasp at back.

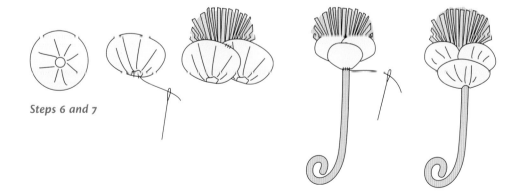

Steps 6 and 7

Acorn

I love to use multiple shades of the same color to add subtle tones to a design. Here, three shades of green felt are layered to resemble an acorn leaf. Seed beads and a thin strip of decorative cord highlight the patterns in the leaf, while acorns—picked from my fall garden—add a whimsical touch.

See templates on page 147.

Pin

1. To make twig, cut a strip of fabric measuring ¾″ × 2″. Turn raw edges under very slightly (about ¹⁄₁₆″). Fold in half lengthwise and overstitch edges together.

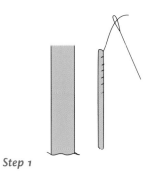

Step 1

SELECTIONS

Pin: felt in three shades of green; fabric scrap

Acorns: four natural acorn shells, silk scraps, and batting or stuffing

Beads: about 170 seed beads

Fine decorative cord: ⅛″ wide or less

Embroidery floss

Sew-on safety clasp

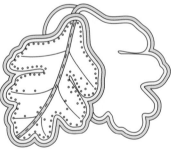

Step 2

2. With templates A and B, cut two each from felt. Position A on top of B, then baste in place Position 4″ strips of decorative cord, wire, or embroidery floss to resemble central vein of each leaf. Stitch in place. Embroider leaf-vein pattern on either side of decorative cord (see stem stitch on page 13). Sew seed beads in place. Overlap leaf pieces as shown and stitch in place. Sew twig to back.

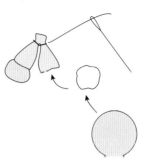

3. With template C, cut one from felt. Position A/B on top of C, then stitch in place, trapping twig between layers. Stitch clasp in place on back of pin.

Acorns

4. Wash acorn shells. Cut and stuff a large enough fabric scrap to fit nicely inside shell, as in photograph. Stitch once or twice to hold stuffing inside fabric. Glue inside shell, then hold stuffed fabric against glue until it sticks. This may take practice to gain a nice, rounded acorn fruit—so have extra acorns on hand! Make four. Wrap embroidery floss around acorn tips, then stitch tight to secure to leaves.

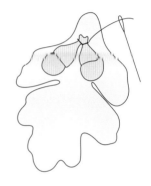

Step 4

SELECTIONS

Pin: silk, cotton, or rayon scraps in at least three
   colors; 10 seed beads

Pouch: cotton and felt scraps

Beads for pouch: about 25 small beads; about
   80 seed beads

Embroidery floss for pouch

Sew-on safety clasp for pin

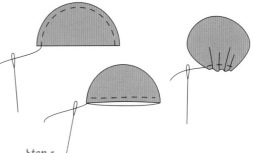

Step 1

Pansy

Sweet and pretty, Pansy pin always raises a smile. Made from silks, cottons, or rayons, it comes together quickly and easily. Add a few seed beads at the center, and it's done. I enjoyed making this little flower pin so much that I had to design a mini-purse to go with it.

See templates on page 148.

Pin

1. With template A, cut 10. Matching contrasting colors and using a scant ⅛″ seam allowance, sew pairs together around curve. Turn right side out. Gather stitch along remaining edge, pulling gathers gently to create petal shape. Backstitch to hold. Make 5.

2. Carefully stitch five petals together along gathered edges to create pansy shape. Sew petals one at a time, as shown.

3. To make yo-yo, cut circle measuring 1¾″ in diameter then follow Step 6 of *Brilliance* on page 59 to complete. Stitch to center front of pansy. Add seed beads to embellish.

4. Cut a circle measuring 1¼″ in diameter. Turn under raw edges by ¼″ and press to hold. Overstitch to center back of pansy. Stitch sew-on clasp in place on this circle.

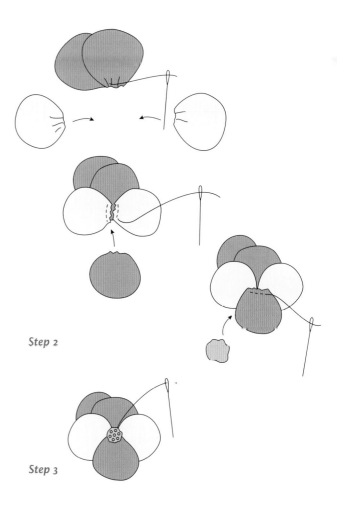

Step 2

Step 3

Pansy *pins are so much fun to make that you will soon have several of them. This simple* Pansy Pouch *is embellished with a finished* Pansy *flower. Make a pin in the same colorway and enjoy wearing them together!*

Pansy Pouch

1. Cut four circles measuring 4″ from felt. Cut two circles measuring 5″ from fabric. Fold in ½″ seam allowances on fabric pieces and press to hold. Slip a felt piece inside folded-in seam allowance of each fabric piece. Sew felt to folded-in seam allowance, taking care not to let needle go through to purse front. Sew completed pansy flower to one of prepared circles. Sew remaining felt pieces to back of each circle.

2. Cut two strips of felt measuring ½″ × 10″. Pin together, then stitch down center, adding seed beads as you go.

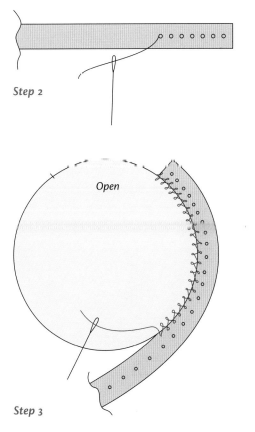

Open

3 Attach one edge of felt strip to pouch back, using herringbone stitch and embroidery thread (see page 12). About 2½" of circle will remain open. Repeat, sewing other edge of felt strip to purse front.

4. Thread needle with embroidery floss and knot. Insert from inside to outside of felt strip at one end of opening in pouch. String beads as desired for about 4½". Insert needle into felt at other end of opening in pouch. Backstitch to hold.

Step 3

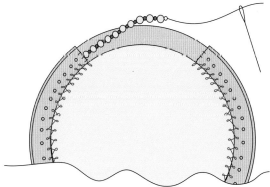

Windmill

This sweet little pin adds a delicate touch of color. Wear it as a unique fashion accessory, or slide a bobby pin through it and Windmill *becomes a pretty hair decoration. You can even add a ribbon loop and turn* Windmill *into a colorful hanging ornament or gift bow.*

Pin

1. Cut nine squares of fabric measuring 2″ × 2″. Fold in half diagonally and pin. Fold again and pin twice as shown.

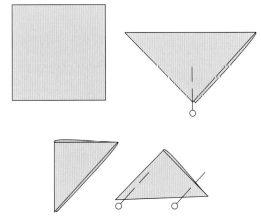

Step 1

SELECTIONS

Fabric: up to three selections of silk or cotton

Beads: seven seed beads

⅛″ ribbon (optional)

Sew-on safety clasp or bobby pin (optional)

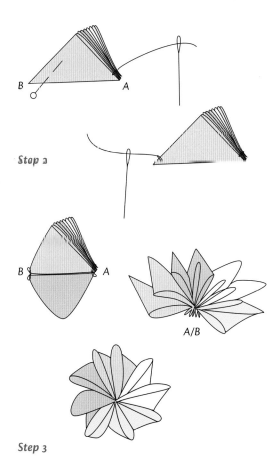

Step 2

2. Layer all nine folded triangles as shown. About ¼″ from tip A, pull knotted thread through layers, one at a time. Stitch to hold. Repeat at tip B.

3. Pull four petals downwards and other petals upwards. Gently separate them to create windmill shape, hiding tips A and B at center. Raw edges of pieces should all be hidden.

4. If desired, make a hanging loop from an 8″ length of ⅛″ silk ribbon. Fold in half and sew ends to center front of windmill.

5. Sew seed beads to center of windmill. If desired, stitch sew-on clasp or bobby pin to back.

A/B

Step 3

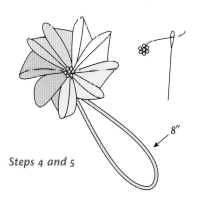

Steps 4 and 5

8″

"Inspiration is a magical sensation. Imagine a million flower petals falling around you, enveloping you in their fragrances. Or picture thousands of soft dandelion seeds as they float on a spring breeze from garden to garden. Inspiration is a sensation that is at once melancholy and joyous, rhythmic and serene."

Sewing Kits, Pin Totes, Thimbles, and More

FOR THOSE OF US who love to sew, there are few more beloved gifts to give or receive than a charming sewing accessory that will keep our needles, pins, threads, and scissors safe and close to hand. A handmade sewing kit, a pincushion, or even a simple thimble crafted from fabric reminds us each time we see it of the love of the person who made it and the care that was taken in its making. What gift could me more personal or more endearing?

Tidy Tote

Sweet and pretty, this little tote will keep your needles, threads, and pins in place from the beginning to the end of a sewing project. Open it up and you'll find a handy pincushion sewn into the base of the tote—no more loose pins, even when you sew on-the-go.

See template on page 148. Use ¼" seam allowance for sewing.

Buds

1. Follow Step 1 of *Tomato Cache* on page 23 to make three buds.

Tote

2. Cut strip of fabric measuring 4½" × 8½"; cut two strips of felt measuring 4" × 8". With template A, cut four from felt; add ¼" seam allowance then cut two from fabric. Fold in ¼" seam allowances on each fabric piece and press to hold. Slip a felt piece inside folded-in seam allowance of its corresponding fabric piece. Sew felt to folded-in seam

SELECTIONS

Tote: decorative cotton; felt in matching color

Flower: silk scraps

Beads: about 40 small beads; large decorative bead or combination of one large, one small, and one seed bead; about 50 seed beads for interior

Cotton stuffing or batting scraps

Embroidery floss

Two snap fasteners

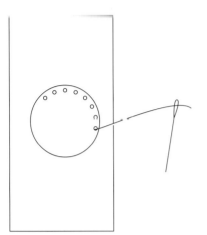

Step 3

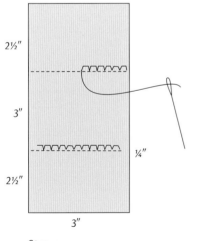

Step 5

allowance, taking care not to let needle go through to tote front.

3. Cut a 2½″ diameter circle from felt. Position at center of remaining felt strip. Sew seed beads in place, stitching through both layers of felt. When about 1″ remains unstitched, stuff tightly with batting to form pincushion. Complete stitching of beads.

4. Position felt strip with pincushion on top of felt-backed fabric strip, with felts next to each other.

5 At dashed lines, pinch about ¼″ fabric only (not felt lining) and, using embroidery floss, blanket-stitch along width of tote, starting and stopping about ¼″ from either end.

6. Position remaining template A pieces on top of felt-backed template A pieces, with felts next to each other. Pin, then use a small overstitch to sew around both pieces, taking care not to allow needle to go through to tote front. Use blanket stitch and embroidery floss to sew sides of tote in place. Sew snap fasteners at top inside corners of tote, stitching through felt only.

Complete

7. Position buds from Step 1 at center front of tote, then sew in place. Attach large bead as in photograph, locking it in place with a small bead and a seed bead. Knot thread and bring from inside to front of tote, immediately to right of right-most bud. String beads onto thread as desired for about 4″, then draw thread from tote front to inside and backstitch to hold. Make another 1″ string of beads and secure one end of it beneath button.

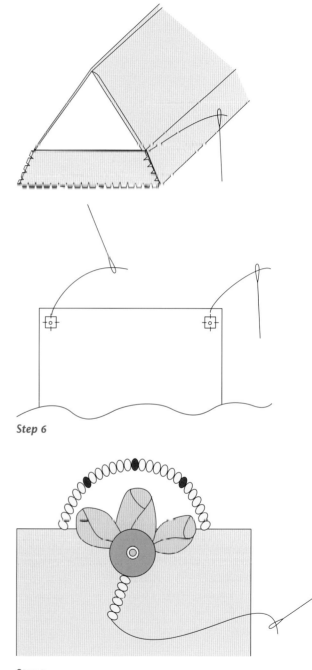

Step 6

Step 7

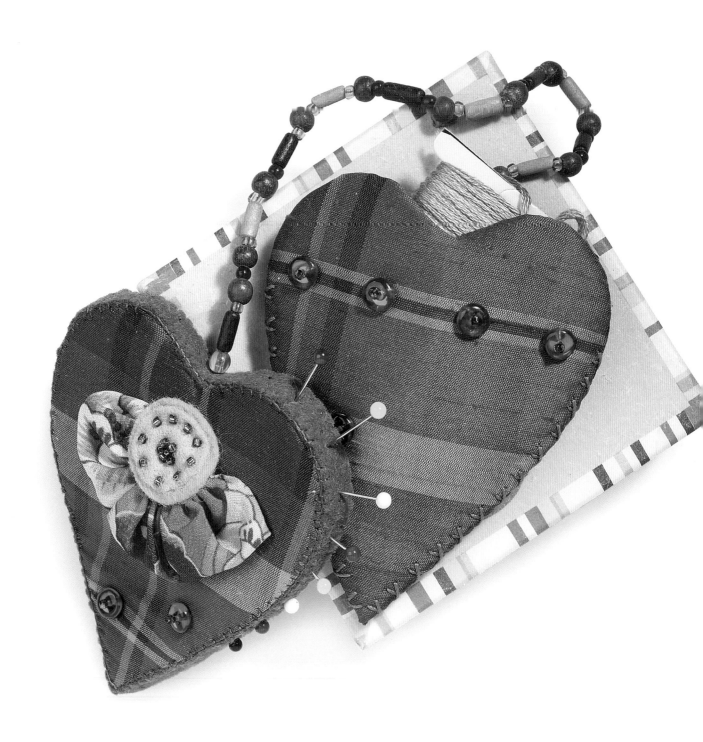

'Ivy 'Pocket

Ivy Pocket *is a simple gift to make by hand and give with all your heart. Imagine a mother's delight when she opens a package on Valentine's Day or Mother's Day to find this lovely thread and pin tote inside. It will hang prettily over a chair arm and take care of her needle and pins as she sews.*

See templates on page 148. Use ¼" seam allowance unless otherwise indicated.

Pocket

1. With template A, cut eight hearts from felt. Add ¼" seam allowance then cut four from fabric. Fold in seam allowances on each fabric piece and press to hold. Slip a felt piece inside folded-in seam allowance of its corresponding fabric piece. Sew felt to folded-in seam allowance, taking care not to let needle go through to pocket front. Trim remaining felt pieces to make them ¹⁄₁₆" or less smaller than others. Position one on top of each felt-backed piece, felt sides touching, then sew in place. Make four.

SELECTIONS

Pocket: fabric and felts in similar tones

Yo-yo: scraps of silk or cotton

Beads: mixture of small beads, bugle beads, and seed beads

Embroidery floss

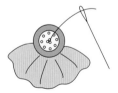

Step 2

2. Cut a circle from cotton or silk, measuring 2¾″ in diameter. Follow step 6 of *Brilliance* on page 59 to make a yo-yo. Fold yo-yo just above center, so that front half is slightly larger than back half. Position about ½″ from top center at front of one of hearts, then stitch in place. Cut two small circles from felt (about ⅞″ and ⅝″ in diameter). Sew together, attaching a circle of seed beads at same time. Sew more beads to center of circles as desired. Sew in place on top of yo-yo. Add more beads as desired to this pocket front.

3. Cut two strips of felt measuring ⅜" × 9½". Place one on top of other, then stitch together. Join ends to make loop. Pin one edge of loop around heart from Step 2, then stitch in place. Stitch another felt-backed heart shape to other edge of loop. Use a simple overstitch or coil stitch (see page 7.) This forms pincushion around perimeter of heart.

4. Use embroidery floss and herringbone stitch to sew remaining two heart shapes together, stopping at points A and leaving top open as shown. Add beads to front of heart shape as desired.

5. String beads as desired to a length of about 6½". Sew ends of bead-string to inside of each heart pocket.

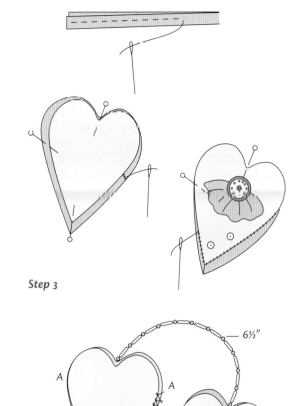

Step 3

Step 4

— 6½"

A   A

柿

Persimmon Pincushion

Everyone who sews needs a variety of pincushions! The pretty persimmon shape is easy to make and is small enough to carry along in your sewing kit.

See template on page 149. Use ¼″ seam allowance for sewing.

Pincushion

1. Cut circle measuring 6½″ in diameter from fabric. Take a running stitch around circumference, stuff with batting, and pull gathering stitches. Stuff until pincushion is very firm. Pull gathers tight and backstitch to hold.

2. Using template A, cut two from felt for calyx. Sew together around perimeter, adding seed beads as you stitch.

SELECTIONS

Pincushion: cotton or silk; felt in contrast color for calyx

Leaf: fabric scrap

Beads: about 50 seed beads

Cotton stuffing or batting scraps

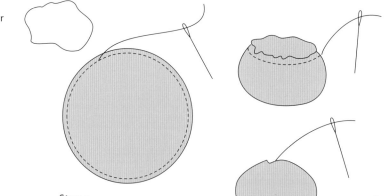

Step 1

Step 2

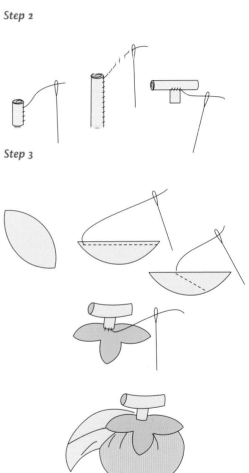

Step 3

3. Cut strip of felt measuring ½″ × 1½″ for short stem. Roll lengthwise and stitch to hold. Repeat with 1½″ square of felt for longer stem. Place longer stem across top of shorter stem and stitch in place. Stitch to calyx, then stitch calyx to top of pincushion.

4. With template B, cut two from fabric for leaf. Right sides together, stitch around perimeter, leaving about 1″ open. Turn right side out. then blind stitch opening closed. To make leaf veins, fold leaf in half lengthwise, then sew very close to folded edge (1⁄16″ or less). Open out, then carefully fold along dashed lines of template. Again, stitch very close to edge. Sew tip of leaf in place at center of calyx.

Step 4

Heian Pin-Pin

This decorative sewing case beautifully combines a soft pincushion with a hide-away for threads, needles, and other small accessories. The colorful embroidery around the sides, as well as the delicate seed beads, add a sophisticated touch.

Use ¼" seam allowance for sewing.

Embroidered Bands

1. Cut four strips measuring ¾" × 9½" from felt; cut two from fabric. Fold in seam allowances on fabric pieces by a scant ⅛" on all sides and press to hold. Position each on top of a corresponding felt piece, then use tiny stitches and matching thread to sew in place. About ⅛" of felt will show behind fabric. Make two.

2. With chalk or other marker, make guide points every inch along top and bottom edges. With embroidery floss and

SELECTIONS

Fabrics: combination of up to three silks or cottons for outside; felt in up to four colors for lining.

Beads: about 350 seed beads

Embroidery floss in multiple colors (up to six)

Stuffing

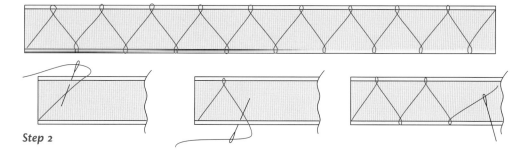

Step 2

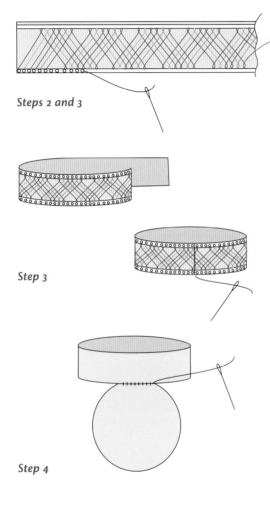

Steps 2 and 3

Step 3

Step 4

herringbone stitch (see page 12), stitch as shown, going from guide points at bottom edge to top edge as shown. Change to another color thread, then repeat, beginning about ⅛" away from first set of stitches. Repeat for a total of six sets.

3. Sew seed beads in place onto felt above and below fabric strip. Position on top of remaining strip of felt, with felt sides touching. Pin, then sew together. For embroidered band at top of Pin-Pin in photograph, allow ⅛" of this new felt piece (green) to show behind first felt piece (yellow). For bottom embroidered band, trim felt (purple) so that it is exactly even with first felt piece (red). Sew ends together to make loop.

Base

4. Cut three 3" diameter circles from felt; cut three 3½" diameter circles from fabric. Fold in ¼" seam allowances on each fabric piece and press to hold. Slip a corresponding felt piece inside folded-in seam allowance of fabric pieces. Set one completed circle aside for top. Sew one completed circle to base of bottom embroidered band as shown. Use a simple overstitch or coil stitch (see page 7). Slip remaining circle inside band and make stitches at 1" intervals around perimeter to attach to base.

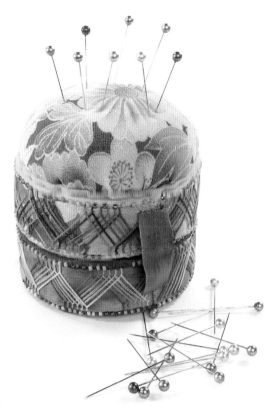

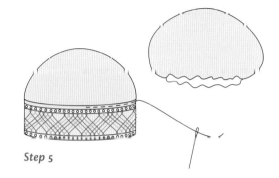

Top

5. Using remaining felt-backed circle from Step 4, overstitch or coil stitch in place around remaining embroidered band to form base of top. Cut 6″ diameter circle from fabric. Pin or baste in place around perimeter of embroidered band. Take out one or two pins, then stuff as full as possible with stuffing, achieving as soft, rounded shape. Sew fabric carefully in place, manipulating shape as you go and stitching through overhanging edge of felt (green in photograph) at top of embroidered band.

6. Cut a 2″ square of fabric. Fold all four sides inwards by about ¼″ and press. Fold in half, then sew around edges as shown. Position then stitch onto top and base as shown.

Step 5

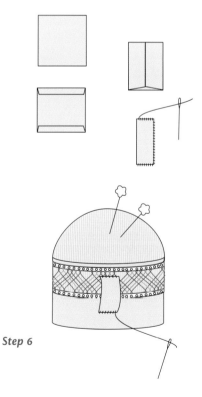

Step 6

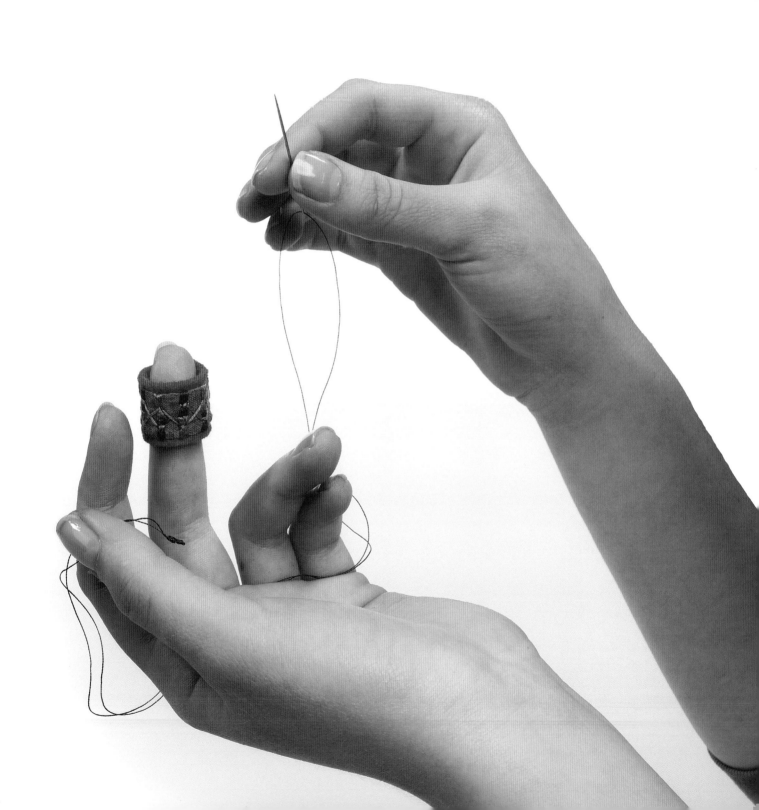

Thimbles!

I like the softness of traditional Japanese thimbles made from fabric. I also find that my thimble finger does not tire as easily as it might with a metal thimble. I love to make these pretty little rings and use them to hold notes or gift tags, as well as for sewing! You might even want to wear them as jewelry for your fingers or toes! I've suggested four embroidery patterns, but you will soon want to create a design of your own.

Use ¼" seam allowance for sewing.

Thimble

Cut a strip of felt measuring ½" × 2¼" and a strip of fabric measuring 1"x 2¾". Test length of felt strip around your finger and adjust size as necessary. Fold in all sides of fabric strip by ¼" and press. Position on top of felt strip, then use small overstitch to sew in place. Draw guidelines to create grid, shown in red in diagrams. Begin embroidery design. Where possible, try to hide back stitches between fabric and felt—there is no need to stitch all way through felt. When embroidery is complete, join ends to make a loop, adjusting size as necessary.

SELECTIONS

Fabrics: Silk or cotton scraps; felt scraps

Embroidery floss: 2-ply in multiple colors

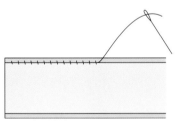

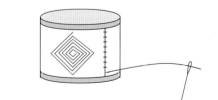

General instructions for all designs

Design A

Design A

With first floss color, make four large stitches from top to bottom of every second grid square as shown. Repeat in alternate grid squares, using second floss color. With third floss color, make a double stitch at center of first set of four threads, grouping threads together to create haystack shape. Cross diagonally. Continue along length of thimble to next set of four threads and repeat.

Design B

Beginning at first point where guidelines cross, embroider a tiny square. Make up to six more squares around this one, each larger than the previous. If desired, switch colors for the final two squares. Repeat along length of fabric.

Design A

Design B

Design B

Design C

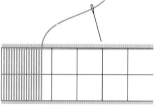

Design C

Make large stitches from to bottom of fabric as shown.
You will need about ten stitches to fill each gird division.
Changing floss color, make a double stitch at center of first
set of threads (between grid lines), grouping threads together
to create haystack shape. Cross to next set of four threads
and repeat. Continue along length of thimble.

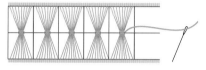

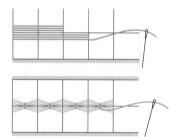

Design C

Design D

Make five large stitches across width of each grid square as
shown. (If desired, use two different colors of floss.) Change
colors, then make a double stitch at center of first set of
threads, grouping threads together to create horizontal
haystack shape. Cross to next set of four threads and repeat.
Continue along length of thimble.

Design D

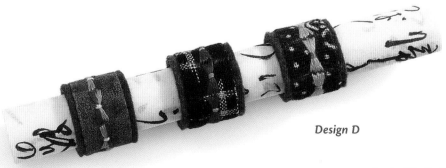

Design D

Mallow Rose

Designed to hold a simple round pincushion, you can use this little fabric bowl for anything you please. It makes a pretty candy dish or it can hold a favorite piece of jewelry while brightening up your dresser.

See templates on page 149. Use ¼″ seam allowance for sewing.

Bowl

1. With template A, cut five from felt; add ½″ seam allowance and cut five from fabric. Fold in seam allowances on each fabric piece and press to hold. Slip a corresponding felt piece inside folded-in seam allowance. Sew felt to folded-in seam allowance, taking care not to let needle go through to front. Make five.

2. With template B, cut five from felt. Position a fabric-wrapped shape from Step 1 on top of each. Sew together as you stitch beads in place. Sew additional beads at top of B pieces.

SELECTIONS

Bowl: cotton or silk; felt in contrast color

Pincushion: silk and felt scraps

Beads: about 600 seed beads

Cotton stuffing or batting scraps

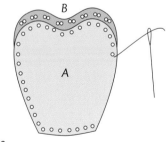

Step 2

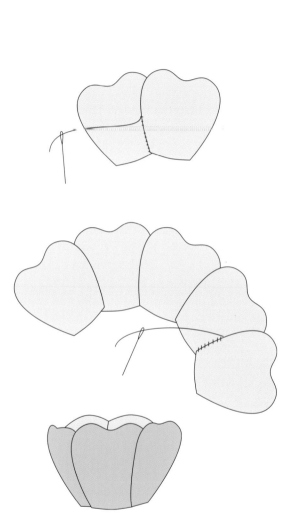

Step 3

3. Overlapping by about ¼″, stitch two completed leaves together, starting at base and stitching for about 1″. Repeat until all five leaves are connected, then stitch last leaf to first in same way.

4. With template C, cut one from felt. Overstitch to bottom of flower piece to create bowl.

Pincushion

5. Cut a 4″ diameter circle from fabric and a ¾″ circle from felt. Gather stitch around perimeter of fabric circle. Stuff with batting then pull gathers to create ball shape. Backstitch to hold. Sew felt circle in place, hiding gathers.

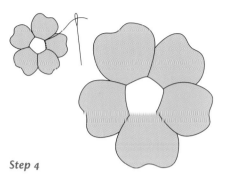

Step 4

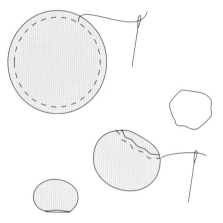

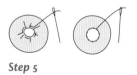

Step 5

Cherry Booklet

Keep you pins safe and your needles organized by size in this leaf-shaped booklet. Hang it in your sewing area and you will always be able to find fresh needles and pins when you need them.

See template on page 130. Use ½" seam allowance for booklet cover only; use ¼" seam allowance for other sewing.

Booklet

1. With template A, cut seven from felt. Add ½" seam allowance, then cut two from fabric. Fold in seam allowances on each fabric piece and press to hold. Slip a felt piece inside folded-in seam allowance of each fabric piece. Sew felt to folded-in seam allowance, taking care not to let needle go through to front. Sew another felt piece on top, hiding fabric seam allowance. (If necessary, trim felt piece so that it is about ⅛" smaller than felt-backed fabric.) Make two.

2. Place remaining three felt pieces between booklet covers. Using embroidery floss and buttonhole stitch, sew through all layers for about 1" along either side of tip.

SELECTIONS

Booklet: silk or cotton; felt in contrast color

Buds: silk, cotton, or felt scraps; silk or cotton scraps for stems and hanging loop

Beads: about 150 seed beads

Cotton stuffing or batting scraps

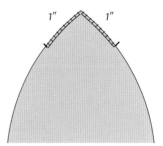

Step 2

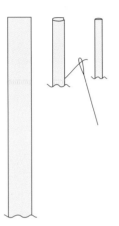

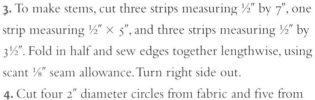

Cherries

3. To make stems, cut three strips measuring ½″ by 7″, one strip measuring ½″ × 5″, and three strips measuring ½″ by 3½″. Fold in half and sew edges together lengthwise, using scant ⅛″ seam allowance. Turn right side out.

4. Cut four 2″ diameter circles from fabric and five from felt. Gather stitch around perimeter. Stuff with batting then pull gathers to create ball shape. Stuff one end of each stem into gathers, then backstitch to hold. Repeat, stuffing other end of longer stems into another cherry. Four stems will

Step 3

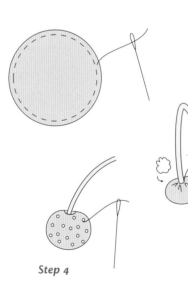

Step 4

now have cherries attached at either end; shortest stem will have a cherry at one end. As desired, sew seed beads to some of cherries

5. Make a loop at top of shortest stem by folding end without cherry over by about ¾" and sewing in place to center of stem. Without cutting thread, sew to tip of front cover of booklet. Fold stems of remaining cherries in half, then sew this center point in place at tip, adjusting lengths of stems as desired.

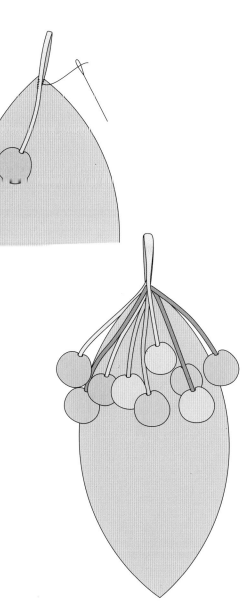

Step 5

"After a long day in my studio, the moon invites me and my little dogs
for an evening stroll. Silver rays break through the cedar and fir trees,
transforming the woods outside my home into a new enchanted
world. My weary soul is bathed in warm moonlight. My heart is
comforted and healed, as if the moon's rays had energized my spirit.
Joy permeates my being and 1 give thanks for the wonderful day."

Pretty, Playful, and Fun to Make

I HAVE ALWAYS LOVED temari, the soft handballs that have been the playthings of Japanese children as well as adults for centuries. This collection includes three of my favorite temari designs, as well as other whimsical items to make for indoor play or as decorative accents. Make them as gifts and they are sure to bring a smile.

Temari

Temari *were traditionally made from remnants of old kimono. Strips of silk were wadded up to make a ball, which was then wound tightly with silk threads. Finally, the ball was decorated with exquisite embroidered patterns. Temari were believed to bring good fortune, with the power to bestow happiness on those who held them.*

Core

Begin by wadding scraps, stuffing, tissue, or newspaper into a tight ball, roughly 3″ in diameter. Wrap ball in piece of fabric. Wrap fabric-covered ball tightly with embroidery floss until you are able to create a nice, round shape. Roll ball to make sure it is smooth and even. Keep wrapping until ball rolls smoothly. Make last several layers using your chosen background color of embroidery floss or perle cotton.

SELECTIONS

Core: dollmaker's stuffing, cotton scraps, gift-wrap tissue, kitchen towel, or newspaper; wrapping fabric; 6-ply embroidery floss #25

Accent: strip of decorative fabric for center ring (for *Rose* and *Kiku*)

6-ply embroidery floss #25: variety of bright colors

Perle cotton (optional)

Wrapping the core

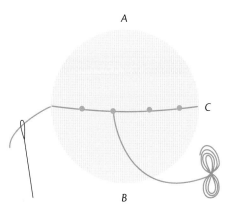

Steps 1 and 2

Finding A, B, and C

To find exact spots A and B, cut a strand of floss to exact same length as circumference of ball. Fold in half then pin midpoint into ball. This is point A. Draw loose ends around ball, inserting second pin where they end. This is point B. Cut strand in half at midpoint, then fold in half again. Loop this new midpoint around pin at point A. Draw loose ends toward center of ball, inserting pin where they end, continue around entire circumference of ball until centerline C is completely marked by pins.

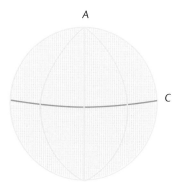

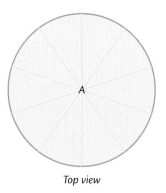

Top view

Step 3

Sakura

1. With pins, mark spots A and B at top and bottom of ball, then centerline C as shown. Sink pins completely into ball so that only pin-heads show. With 3-ply embroidery floss (split from 6-ply), stitch around entire centerline C, making a stable guideline. Remove pins from centerline.

2. Position ten pins evenly around circumference of ball on centerline, dividing ball into ten equal segments. If needed, use a flexible tape measure to help achieve equidistant placement. (For instance, if the circumference of your ball is 10″, pins will be placed exactly 1″ apart.)

3. Knot thread then enter needle into ball about ½″ away from A, exiting at pin head. Do no remove pin. Tug thread to "pop" knot into ball. Draw thread toward B. Make a stitch at one of centerline pins, then continue to B and secure. Do not cut thread. Continue around ball, drawing same thread from B, stitching at centerline, and bringing thread back to A to secure. Do this four more times, drawing floss to a new

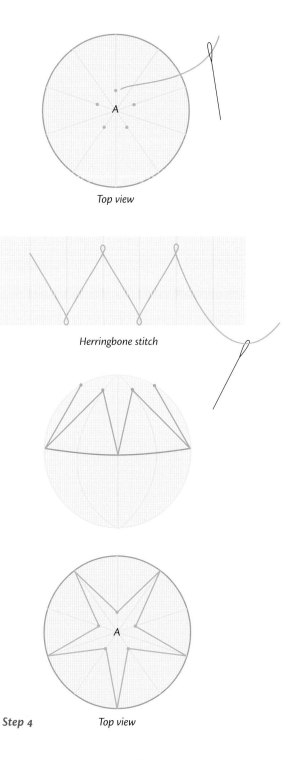

Top view

Herringbone stitch

Step 4   Top view

centerline pin each time. These guidelines now divide ball into ten equal segments. Remove pins.

4. Measure about ½″ down from A along every second guideline and place pin (five pins in all). Changing floss color, hide knot and exit needle at one of pins, as before. Draw thread downwards and diagonally to right, inserting needle immediately to right of intersection of closest guideline and centerline. (Enter needle at or immediately below and to right of centerline.) Make small stitch, coming up immediately to left of same guideline. Draw thread back up and diagonally to right, stopping immediately to right of marking pin on closest guideline. Make small stitch, coming up immediately to left of same guideline. (You are making, in effect, a large herringbone stitch, as shown.) Continue stitching up and down all around ball. Viewed from top, this first round of stitches creates a five-pointed star pattern. Do not cut thread.

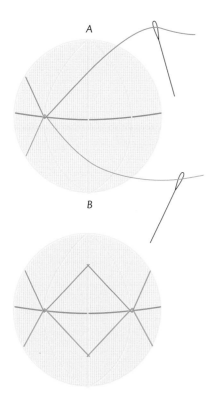

A

B

Step 5

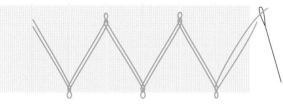

Step 6

Temari Sakura Variation

This variation (see photo, right) uses the same basic pattern as Sakura. This time, the star points are made up of twenty rounds of stitching instead of eleven. Instead of extending only ¼″ below the centerline, threads extend further, with the last one a full inch below the centerline. This results in the oversize triangles above and below the centerline. The large triangles combine to make squares around the centerline.

5. Thread new needle with new color floss. Turn ball over. Repeat Step 4, this time beginning about ½″ down from point B. As before, make a small stitch at centerline, entering needle at immediate right of guideline and exiting at immediate left. Thread new color behind first color, making sure threads cross, as shown. Continue pattern around entire ball. Do not cut thread.

6. For next round, turn ball over and pick up first needle again. Draw thread downwards and diagonally to right (parallel to and lying at left of first stitch). Insert needle immediately to right of closest guideline and slightly below (about ¹⁄₁₆″ or less) centerline. Make a small stitch, coming up immediately to left of same guideline. Draw thread back up and diagonally to right (parallel to and lying at right of first stitch). Stop immediately to right of marking pin, but slightly below (about ¹⁄₁₆″ or less) exit point of first stitch. Take a small stitch under and around threads of previous stitches, and come up immediately to left of same guideline. (By wrapping threads around previous stitches, you are creating a braided effect, as seen in photo on page 105.) Continue around ball.

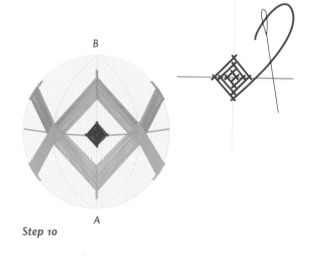

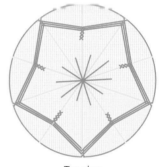

7. Turn ball over and pick up second needle. Repeat Step 6 taking care to cross threads at centerline as before.

8. Repeat Steps 6 and 7 nine more times, for a total of eleven rounds. Flower pattern is complete. You will have a five-pointed star with eleven strands of floss in each star point.

9. Choose new color floss. Make 1″ stitches starting at point A and ending in between original guidelines. There will be a total of ten stitches, creating star shape at top of ball. Repeat at point B.

10. With new color floss, embroider squares at unstitched intersections along centerline. Hide knot at point where threads cross on centerline, then begin by embroidering a tiny square. Make seven or eight squares outside but tightly up against this first one. Make each square larger than the last, so that embroidered area finishes at about ½″ × ½″. Repeat until all five unstitched intersections are covered.

Steps 8 and 9

Top view

Step 10

B

A

Step 1

Step 2

Rose

1. Make core (see page 103). Cut strip of decorative fabric measuring 1½″ × 9″. With regular sewing thread to match fabric, stitch securely around center of ball, and at top and bottom as shown, overlapping ends.

2. Follow Steps 1 and 2 of *Sakura* on page 104 to make centerline and guidelines. This time, make eight evenly spaced guidelines, not ten.

3. Beginning at A, embroider a tiny square, weaving over and under alternating guideline threads (over A, B, C, D, under E, F, G, H). Make seven or eight squares outside and very close

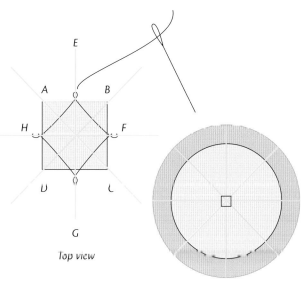

Step 3

Top view

Top view

to this one, each larger than last, until embroidered area is about ½″ × ½″.

4. Change thread color, then start new set of squares, off-set around previous set. Repeat with five or six more colors, and increasing the size of the square by about ½″ with each thread change. Tie off thread once amount of fabric visible at center of ball measures about ½″ at its narrowest point and 1″ at its widest point.

5. Turn ball over and repeat Steps 3 and 4, this time starting at B.

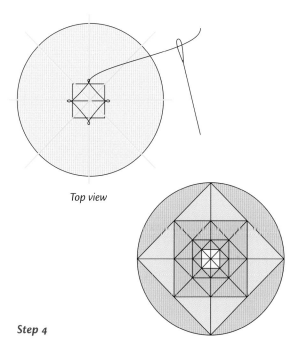

Top view

Step 4

Top view

Step 1

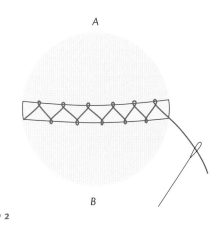

Step 2

Kiku

1. Make core (see page 103). Follow Steps 1 and 2 of *Sakura* on page 104 to make centerline and guidelines. This time, make 16 evenly spaced guidelines, not ten.

2. Cut a ribbon or fabric strip measuring 1″ × 10″. Adjust as necessary to fit circumference of your ball. Fold under raw edges by ¼″ and press. Sew in place around centerline. With 6-ply floss, use herringbone stitch to embroider as shown, beginning at guideline at top edge of ribbon, drawing thread diagonally to right, and ending at guideline at bottom edge of ribbon. (Note that you are securing your stitches *in the ball* immediately above and below the ribbon, *not* into the ribbon itself.)

3. Measure about ½″ down from A along every guideline and place pin (sixteen pins in all). Changing floss color, hide knot and exit needle at one of guideline pins. Draw thread downwards and diagonally to right, inserting needle immediately to right of intersection of closest guideline and edge of ribbon or fabric strip. Make small stitch, coming up immediately to left of same guideline. Draw thread back up and diagonally to right, stopping immediately to right of marking pin on closest guideline. Make small stitch, coming up immediately to left of same guideline. (Unlike Step 6 of *Sakura* on page 106, this time there is no need to cross threads at centerline). Continue pattern around entire ball. Do not cut thread.

4. Repeat Step 3, this time beginning ¾″ down from point A (about ¼″ below previous starting point). Continue around ball. Repeat five more times, each round beginning ¼″ below previous, for a total of seven rounds.

5. If desired, change thread color. Repeat Steps 3 and 4, this time beginning at a new, unstitched guideline. Make a total of five rounds (not seven).

6. Turn ball over and repeat entire pattern (Steps 3 to 5), beginning at point B.

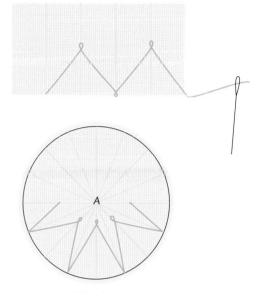

Step 3   **Top view**

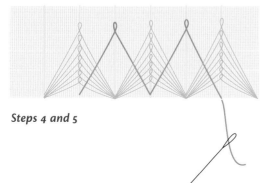

Steps 4 and 5

HINAGAT·KIMONO

晴
着

SELECTIONS

Kimono: silk or lightweight cotton
with rich decorative pattern

Lining: complimentary silk

Cotton stuffing or batting scraps

Embroidery floss

Small tassels (optional)

Miniature Kimono

In past years, many sewing enthusiasts have asked me to publish a pattern for a doll kimono. I have dressed several of my Japanese dolls using this simple design. The red kimono shown on page 114 measures about 6½" in length; the blue kimono opposite is about an inch longer. It is easy to add extra length to fit the doll who will wear your kimono (for most small, decorative dolls there is no need to add to the width or the sleeve size). Look for beautiful decorative silks or cottons that drape well.

See template on page 151. Use scant ⅛" seam allowance for sewing.

Kimono

1. Cut rectangle of fabric measuring 4" × 14½", which includes ⅛" seam allowance. (If desired, add to length to fit your doll.) With template A on fold, cut two from fabric for sleeves. Cut identical pieces from complementary fabric for kimono lining and sleeve linings.

2. Fold rectangles for kimono and lining in half lengthwise and press lightly to mark center line (shoulder line). As shown on diagram, carefully cut along dotted line at center front, stopping at shoulder line. Turn scissors and cut ½" into shoulder line on both sides to create neckline.

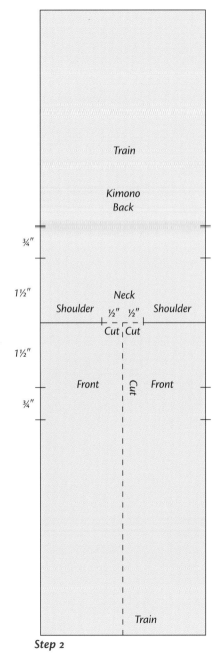

Step 2

3. For front panels, cut two strips measuring 1⅝″ × 6⅛″ from kimono fabric and from lining fabric. Right sides together, position panel on top of kimono front, aligning along bottom edge. Pin then sew in place along long seam only. Open out and press. Repeat for second panel, plus both lining panels.

4. Leaving 2¼″ open at top for armholes, pin then sew side seams, attaching kimono front to back. Repeat for lining. With lining only, lay about ½″ of scrap batting or cotton stuffing along length of hem. Turn in ¼″ hem and stay stitch in place.

5. Align kimono and lining pieces right sides together and pin. Sew around perimeter, leaving bottom hems open. Turn right side out and press. Turn kimono hem under by ½″, then use tiny overstitch to sew kimono hem to stay-stitched lining hem. About ¼″ of stuffed lining will show below kimono hem.

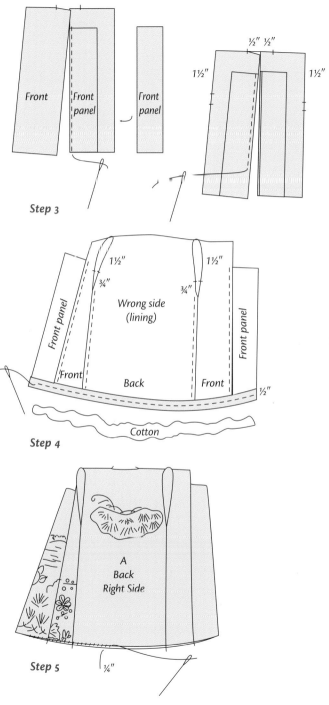

Step 3

Step 4

Step 5

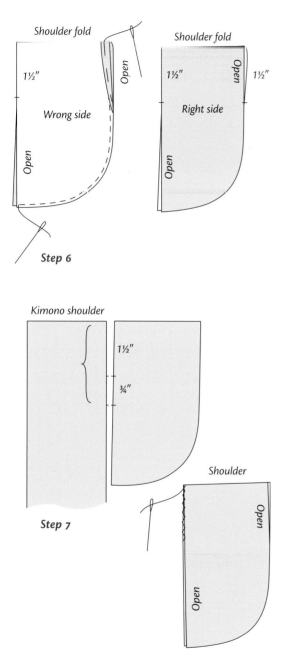

Step 6

Step 7

Sleeves

6. Fold sleeves in half lengthwise and press gently to mark center. Wrong side out, sew around curve, stopping 1½″ from top. Fold in hems around opening and, if desired, press or stay stitch to hold in place. Repeat with lining. Right sides together, sew sleeve pieces to lining pieces around perimeter, leaving about 1″ unstitched. Turn right side out, press, then blindstitch opening closed.

7. Position sleeve at shoulder, with sleeve overlapping by about ⅛″. Use tiny overstitch to sew in place (about 1½″ from top at front and back). Note that there will be an opening of about ¾″ on kimono, beneath sleeve. Kimono belt will loop through here.

Collar and belt

8. Cut strip measuring 1½″ × 14″ for collar. Fold in half lengthwise, right side out, and press. Pin one long edge on a diagonal to kimono front, beginning about 3″ from bottom right, reaching around neckline, and ending about 3″ from bottom left. Adjust as necessary for even placement. Sew

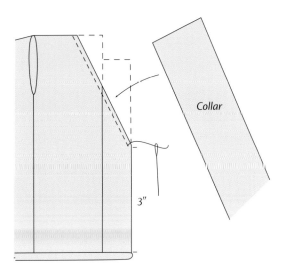

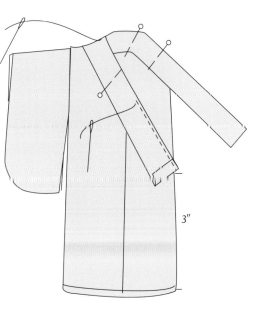

Step 8

strip in place. Fold other edge to inside, encasing excess fabric. Turn in ⅛″ seam allowance and overstitch to lining. Overstitch short collar-ends together.

9. For belt, cut two strips of fabric measuring 1½″ × 9″. Fold lengthwise, press, then sew from end to end. Turn tube right side out. Turn in raw edges at ends and overstitch in place. Make two. Use decorative embroidery stitch and embroidery floss to attach one end of each tube at center front of collar, about 2½″ from collar bottom. If desired, sew small tassels to other ends of belt.

10. To improve drape, make ⅛″ tucks at shoulders as shown, extending about 1½″ down front and back.

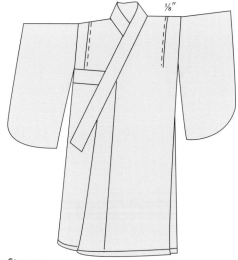

Step 10

Otedama

These traditional Japanese juggling balls are filled with azuki beans, giving them a very pleasant, light feel in the hand. Pretty as paperweights, I like to let my fingers play with otedama while my mind is working out solutions to design problems.

Use scant ⅛" seam allowance for sewing.

Beanbag

1. Cut four strips of fabric measuring 1½" × 3". Using scant ⅛" seam allowance, sew together to midpoints in arrangement shown.

2. Begin sewing remaining sides together. When one side remains unsewn, fill bag with about five teaspoons of beans. The bag should feel about half full. Sew opening closed.

3. Attach a button to top center.

SELECTIONS

Beanbag: silk or cotton scraps

Filling: azuki beans or similar small beans or craft beads

Craft button

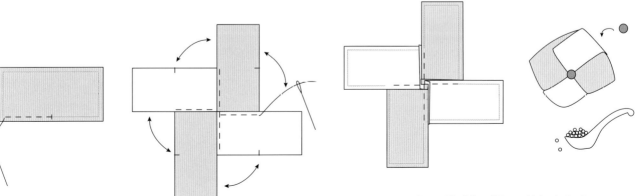

Fishie Pouch

This cheery fish makes a cute cache in the guest room to hold the personal items visitors need during their stay. You might also use it as a desk accessory, keeping your pens, pencils, and letter opener in place. The flower embellishments are easy to make, and the beading highlights the fabric while adding extra sparkle to Fishie's fins and tail.

See templates on pages 152–153. Use ½" seam allowance for purse pieces only; use ⅛" seam allowance for other sewing.

Buds

1. With template D, cut three from each of two fabrics. Pairing contrasting fabrics, sew together around top curve only. Turn right side out and press. Fold in sequence shown, then stitch and gather through all layers at bottom edge. Backstitch to hold. With template E, cut three from felt for calyx. Clip to create fringe as shown. Wrap around bud and stitch in place.

Pouch

2. With template A, cut four from felt. Reserve two for lining and trim ⅛" around entire perimeter of other two

SELECTIONS

Pouch fabric: decorative cotton

Lining: felt in two contrast colors

Buds: cotton or silk scraps; felt for calyx

Beads: thirteen 1" bugle beads; about 90 small beads; about 80 seed beads

Embroidery floss

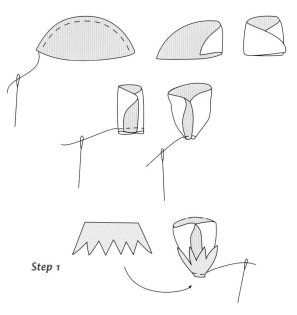

Step 1

pieces. Add ½″ seam allowance to template A, then cut one from fabric for purse back. With template B, cut one from felt. Add ½″ seam allowance to template B then cut one from fabric for purse front. Fold in seam allowances on each fabric piece and press to hold. Slip a corresponding felt piece inside folded-in seam allowance of fabric pieces A and B (use one of trimmed felt pieces for A). Sew felt to folded-in seam allowance, taking care not to let needle go through to fabric front.

3. Sew felt-backed A piece to an untrimmed felt A piece, taking care not to let stitches show on fabric. In same way, sew felt-backed B to remaining trimmed felt A piece to form cache front. Arrange then sew beads and buds from

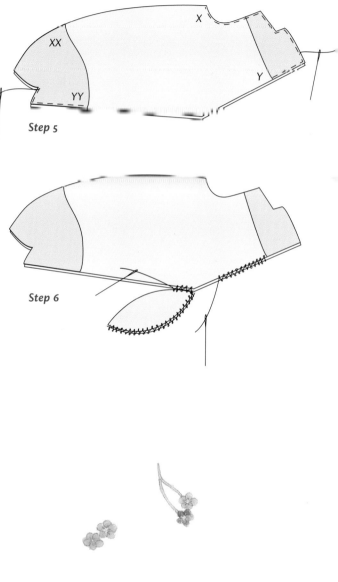

Step 5

Step 6

Step 1 onto cache front, using photograph as guide. Sew this finished piece onto remaining untrimmed felt A.

4. With template C, cut two from felt. Add ½″ seam allowance to template, then cut one from fabric. Fold in seam allowances on fabric piece, then slip a felt piece inside folded-in seam. Sew felt to folded-in seam allowance, taking care not to let needle go through to fabric front. Sew this felt-backed piece to remaining felt piece to complete fish base.

5. Leaving about 3″ open at top, sew fish front to fish back. Starting at right of opening (point *X* on diagram), begin sewing front and back of cache together. (You need only stitch through untrimmed felt pieces, about ⅛″ inwards from edge.) Stitch around tail, stopping at point *Y* on diagram. Next, begin at left of opening (point *XX*) and sew around fish head, stopping at point *YY*.

6. Stitch base into opening at bottom of fish using embroidery floss and herringbone stitch (see page 12). As additional embellishment, continue herringbone stitch along diagonal as shown.

Dragonfly Cache

Fabrics, felts, beading, and embroidery combine to make this sweet dragonfly design. The beaded handle makes it easy to hang the cache around a dresser doorknob, where you might use it to hold a scented bouquet or to hide away keepsakes. The handle also wraps nicely around the wrist, turning Dragonfly Cache into an eye-catching wristlet.

See templates on page 154. Use ½″ seam allowance for purse pieces only; use ¼″ seam allowance for other sewing

Wings and Tailpiece

1. With template B, cut eight from felt. Add ½″ seam allowance, then cut four from fabric. Fold in seam allowances on each fabric piece and press to hold. Slip a corresponding felt piece inside folded-in seam allowance. Sew felt to folded-in seam allowance, taking care not to let needle go through to front fabric. Sew felt-backed piece to each of remaining felt pieces. Complete four wings.

2. Cut strip of felt measuring 1¼″ × 8″. Follow Step 2 of *Camellia Cozy* on page 27 to make tailpiece, leaving about 4½″ uncurled.

SELECTIONS

Purse fabric: cotton or silk

Lining: felt in contrast color

Wings: cotton or silk; felt in contrast color

Tailpiece: felt

Beads: two large for eyes; combination of about 50 small beads for handle

Embroidery floss

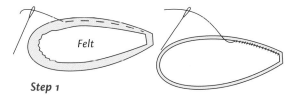

Felt

Step 1

Cache

3. With template A, cut four from felt. Add ½″ seam allowance, then cut two from fabric. Fold in seam allowances on each fabric piece and press to hold. Slip a corresponding felt piece inside folded-in seam allowance. Sew felt to folded-in seam allowance, taking care not to let needle go through to front fabric.

4. Position then stitch wings onto cache front as shown. Sew tailpiece in place, then attach large beads for eyes.

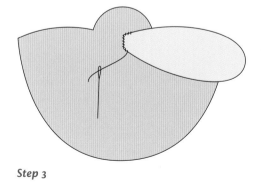

Step 3

5. Using a tiny overstitch, sew remaining two felt A pieces to back and front of purse, forming lining.

6. Wrong sides together and leaving top open, sew around entire curve using embroidery floss and herringbone stitch (see page 12). String beads for handle. Attach one end to left front of dragonfly head; attach other end to right back of dragonfly head as shown.

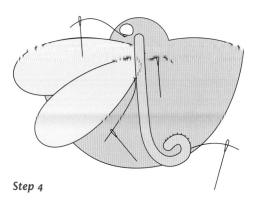

Step 4

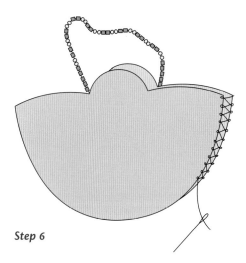

Step 6

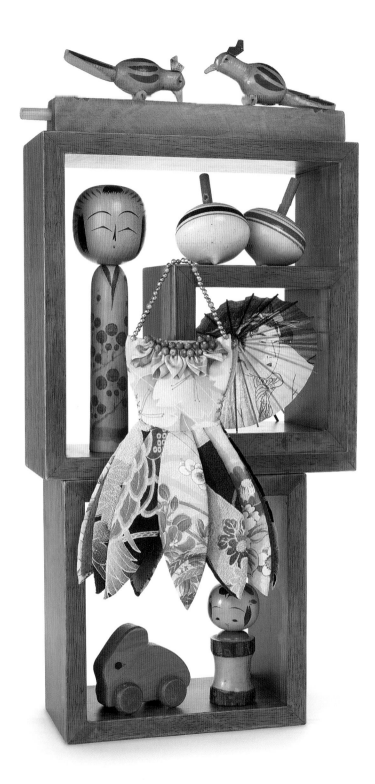

Aloha

This pretty dancing girl makes a lovely spring or summer accent. Let her care of a special item of jewelry for you. Easy to make and fun to embellish, Aloha has an inside pocket deep enough to hold a bottle of cologne or a lavender sachet.

See templates on page 155. Use ½" seam allowance for pouch pieces only; use ¼" seam allowance for other sewing.

Buds and Skirt

1. Cut five circles measuring 2" from silk. Follow Step 1 of *Tomato Cache* on page 23 to make five buds.

2. With template B, cut 20 from felt. Add ½" seam allowance, then cut 10 from fabric. Fold in seam allowances on each fabric piece and press to hold. Slip a corresponding felt piece inside folded-in seam allowance. Sew felt to folded-in seam allowance, taking care not to let needle go through to front fabric. Sew felt-backed piece to each of remaining felt pieces.

SELECTIONS

Purse fabric: cotton or silk

Lining: felt

Skirt: cotton or silk; felt two or more colors

Buds: silk scraps

Beads: 23 small beads and 23 seed beads for neckband; two large beads and about 40 seed beads for handle

Embroidery floss

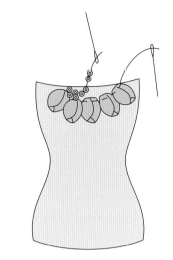

Step 4

2¼″

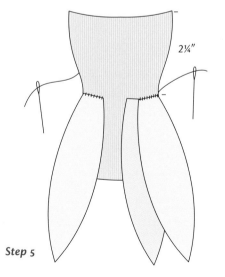

Step 5

Pouch

3. With template A, cut four from felt. Add ½″ seam allowance, then cut two from fabric. Fold in seam allowances on each fabric piece and press to hold. Slip a corresponding felt piece inside folded-in seam allowance. Sew felt to folded-in seam allowance, taking care not to let needle go through to front fabric.

4. Position then sew buds to pouch front. Attach 18 small beads, locking each in place with a seed bead. In same way, attach five small beads and five seed beads to pouch back.

5. Position then stitch five skirt pieces each onto pouch front and back. Using a tiny overstitch, sew remaining two felt A pieces to pouch front and back, forming lining.

6. Wrong sides together and leaving about 1½″ open at top of each side, sew around rest of pouch using embroidery floss and herringbone stitch (see page 12).

7. String beads for handle. Begin with small, secure backstitch through right-hand corner of back pouch, bringing thread out at inside lining; string large bead, then draw thread through to purse pouch front; continue threading small beads for about 5″, then draw thread through to left-hand corner of pouch front; add another large bead, then exit through pouch back and backstitch to hold.

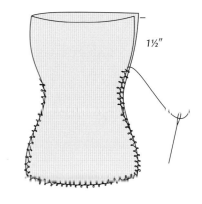

Step 6

Step 7

Cicada

A sound that never fails to awake memories of my childhood in Japan is the soft click-click of cicada wings on a warm summer night. Tuck some change inside and loop this little fellow around a belt as a dazzling accessory. Or use Cicada *as a keepsake pouch, hanging gracefully on a bedroom wall.*

See templates on page 156. Use ½" seam allowance for purse pieces only; use ¼" seam allowance for other sewing.

Wings

1. With template B, cut eight from felt. Add ½" seam allowance, then cut four from fabric. Fold in seam allowances on each fabric piece and press to hold. Slip a

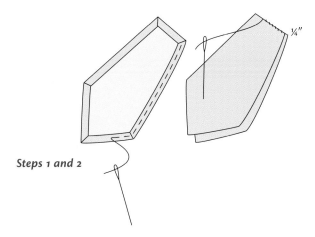

Steps 1 and 2

SELECTIONS

Purse fabric: cotton or silk

Lining: felt in matching color

Wings: cotton or silk; felt in contrast color

Beads: two large beads for eyes; four 1" cylindrical beads; combination of about 30 small beads for handle

Embroidery floss

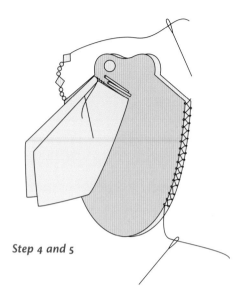

Step 4 and 5

corresponding felt piece inside folded-in seam allowance. Sew felt to folded-in seam allowance, taking care not to let needle go through to front fabric. Sew felt-backed piece to each of remaining felt pieces. Complete four wings.

2. Position first pair of wing pieces as shown, offset at top edge by about ¼″. Use small overstitch to sew together along top edge. Repeat, making a mirror-image pair from remaining wing pieces.

Pouch

3. With template A, cut four from felt. Add ½″ seam allowance, then cut two from fabric. Fold in seam allowances

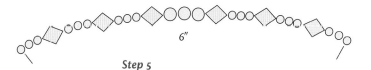

Step 5

6"

on each fabric piece and press to hold. Slip a corresponding felt piece inside folded-in seam allowance. Sew felt to folded-in seam allowance, taking care not to let needle go through to front fabric.

4. Position then stitch wings onto pouch front as shown. Attach two large beads and four cylindrical beads as shown. Using a small overstitch, sew remaining two felt A pieces to back and front of purse, forming lining.

5. Wrong sides together and leaving top open, sew around entire curve using embroidery floss and herringbone stitch (see page 12). String beads to make a 6" handle. Attach ends of handle at tops of sewn curve.

Bird of Paradise see pages 16–21

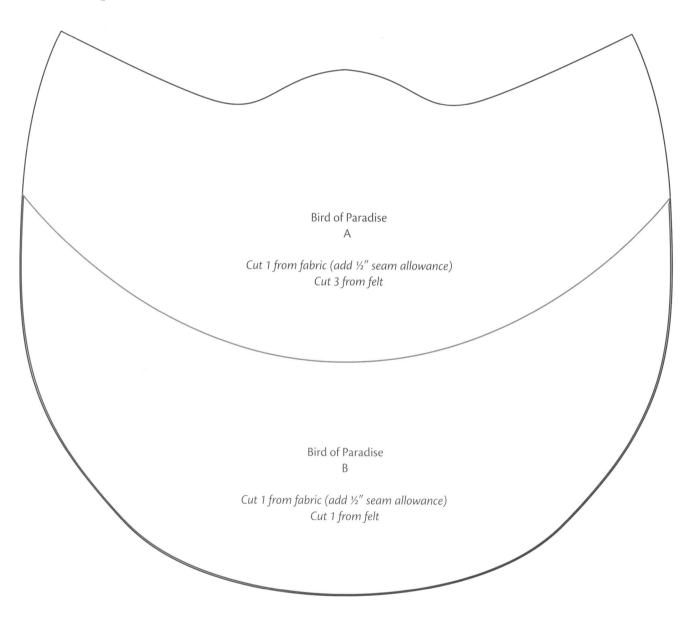

Bird of Paradise
A

Cut 1 from fabric (add ½" seam allowance)
Cut 3 from felt

Bird of Paradise
B

Cut 1 from fabric (add ½" seam allowance)
Cut 1 from felt

Bird of Paradise see pages 16–21

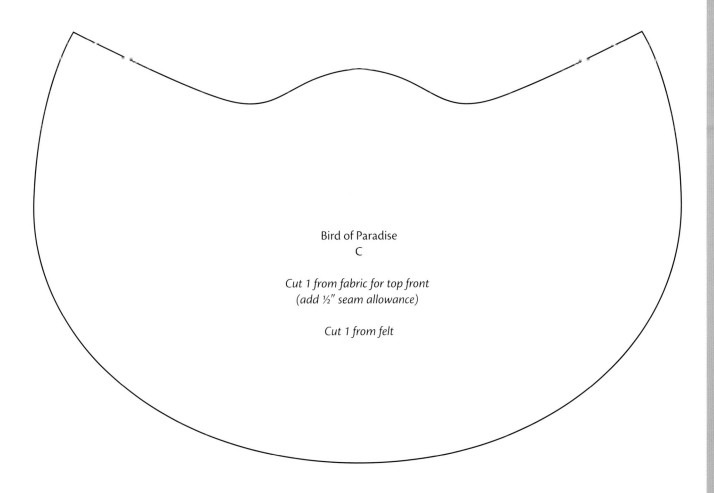

Bird of Paradise
C

Cut 1 from fabric for top front
(add ½" seam allowance)

Cut 1 from felt

Tomato Cache *see pages 22–25*

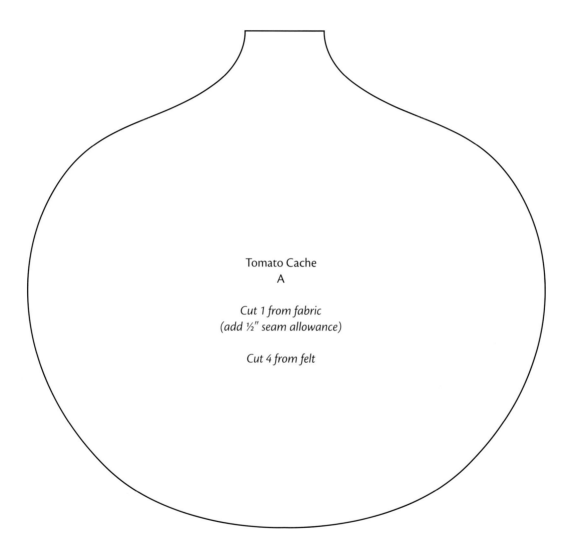

Tomato Cache
A

*Cut 1 from fabric
(add ½" seam allowance)*

Cut 4 from felt

Tomato Cache see pages 22–25

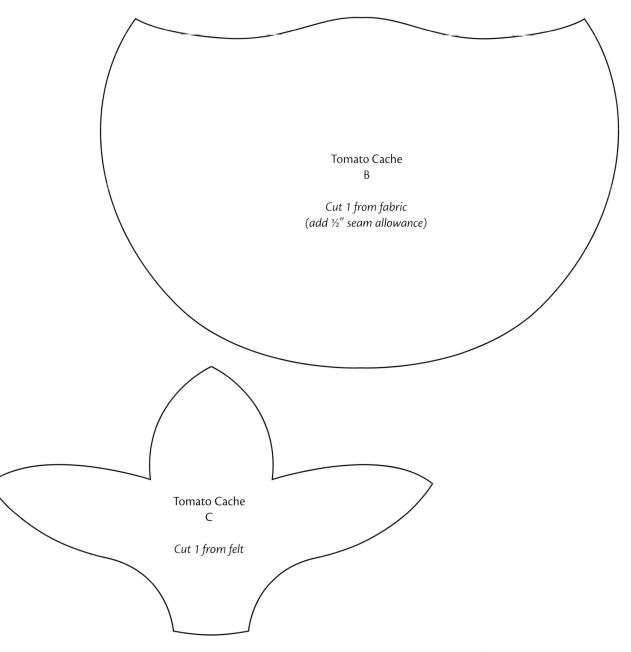

Tomato Cache
B

Cut 1 from fabric
(add ½" seam allowance)

Tomato Cache
C

Cut 1 from felt

Camellia Cozy see pages 26–29

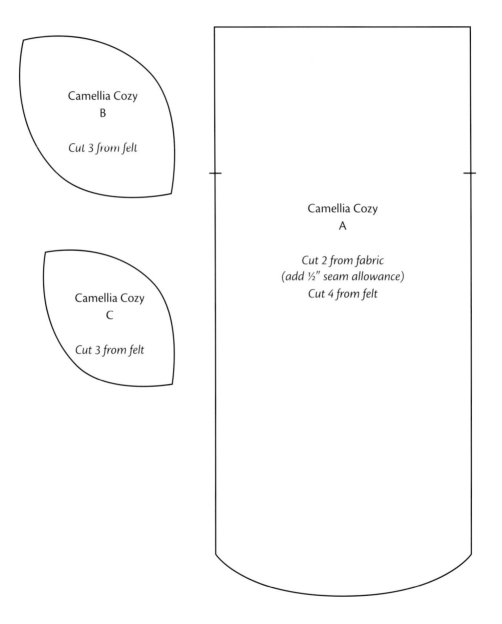

Camellia Cozy
B

Cut 3 from felt

Camellia Cozy
C

Cut 3 from felt

Camellia Cozy
A

*Cut 2 from fabric
(add ½" seam allowance)
Cut 4 from felt*

Posy Wristlet see pages 30–33

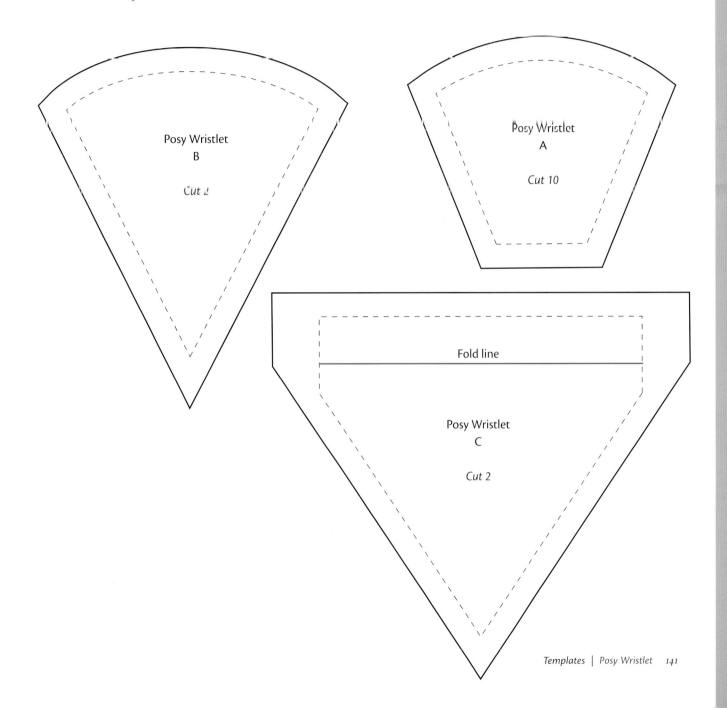

Posy Wristlet
B

Cut 2

Posy Wristlet
A

Cut 10

Fold line

Posy Wristlet
C

Cut 2

Evening Elegance

see pages 34–37

Evening Elegance
A

Cut 1 from fabric
(add ½" seam allowance)

Cut 4 from felt

Evening Elegance
B

Cut 1 from fabric
(add ½" seam allowance)

Evening Elegance see pages 34–37

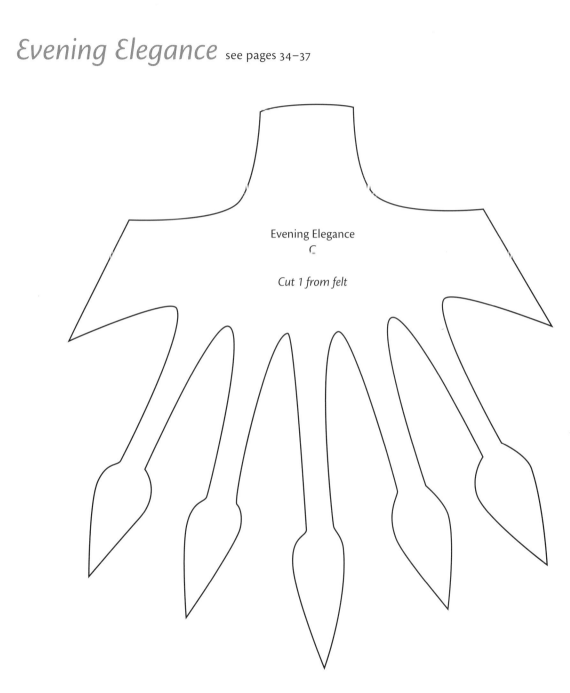

Evening Elegance

Cut 1 from felt

Kara Lily Caddy see pages 42–45

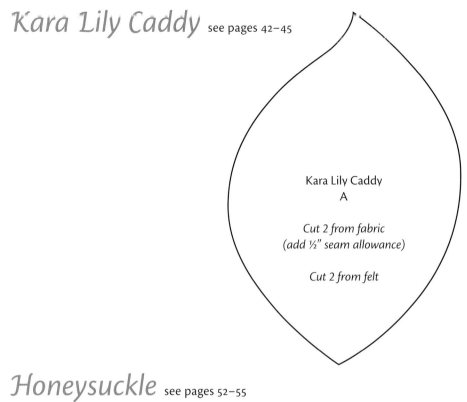

Kara Lily Caddy
A

Cut 2 from fabric
(add ½" seam allowance)

Cut 2 from felt

Honeysuckle see pages 52–55

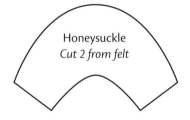

Honeysuckle
Cut 2 from felt

Apple Pocket see pages 46–49

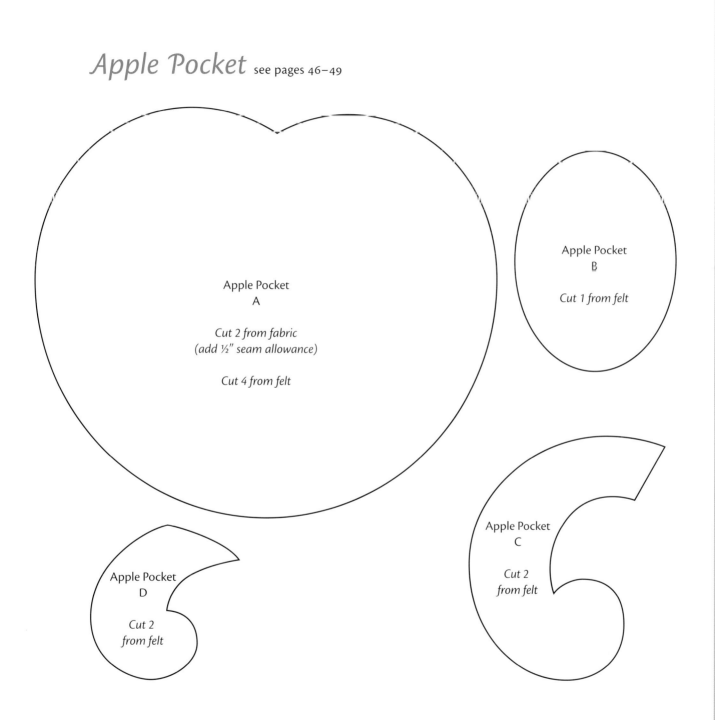

Apple Pocket
A

Cut 2 from fabric
(add ½" seam allowance)

Cut 4 from felt

Apple Pocket
B

Cut 1 from felt

Apple Pocket
C

Cut 2
from felt

Apple Pocket
D

Cut 2
from felt

Brilliance see pages 56–59

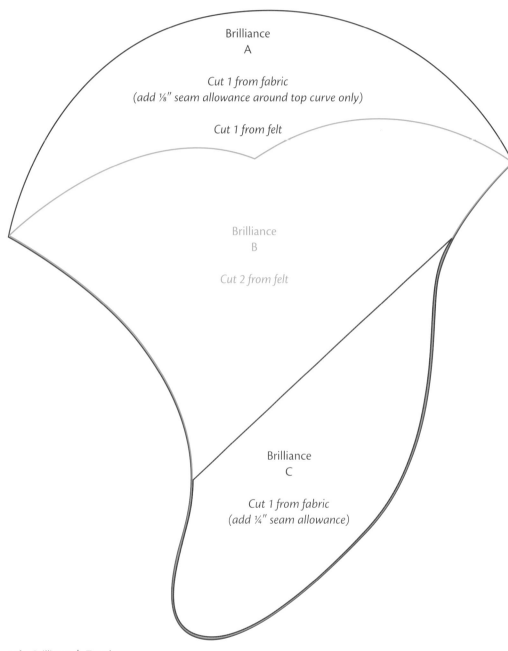

Brilliance
A

Cut 1 from fabric
(add ⅛" seam allowance around top curve only)

Cut 1 from felt

Brilliance
B

Cut 2 from felt

Brilliance
C

Cut 1 from fabric
(add ¼" seam allowance)

Acorn see pages 60–63

Acorn
A

Cut 2 from felt

Acorn
B

Cut 2 from felt

Acorn
C

Cut 1 from felt

Pansy *see pages 64–67*

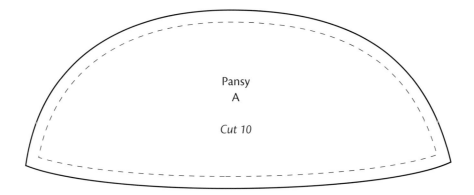

Pansy
A

Cut 10

Tidy Tote *see pages 74–77*

Tidy
Tote
A

Cut 2
from fabric
(add ¼"
seam
allowance)

Cut 4
from felt

Ivy Pocket *see pages 78–81*

Ivy Pocket
A

Cut 4 from fabric
(add ¼" seam allowance)

Cut 8 from felt

Persimmon Pincushion see pages 82–83

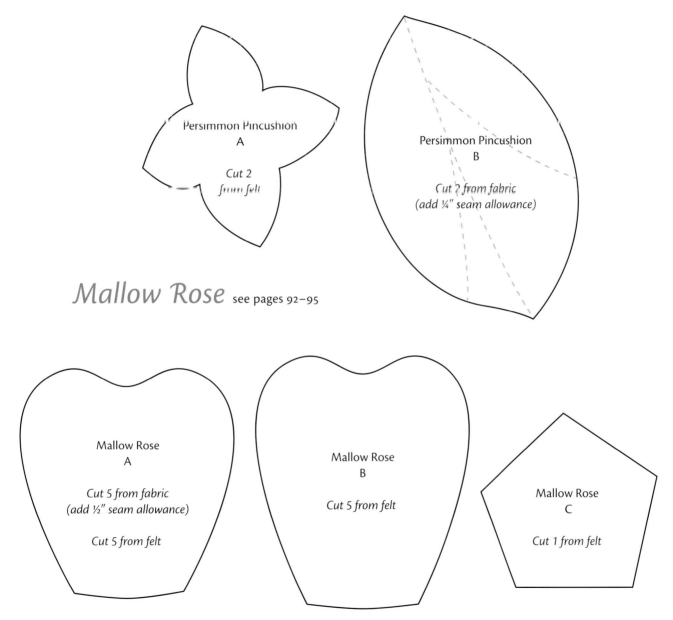

Persimmon Pincushion
A

Cut 2
from felt

Persimmon Pincushion
B

Cut 2 from fabric
(add ¼" seam allowance)

Mallow Rose see pages 92–95

Mallow Rose
A

Cut 5 from fabric
(add ½" seam allowance)

Cut 5 from felt

Mallow Rose
B

Cut 5 from felt

Mallow Rose
C

Cut 1 from felt

Cherry Booklet *see pages 96–99*

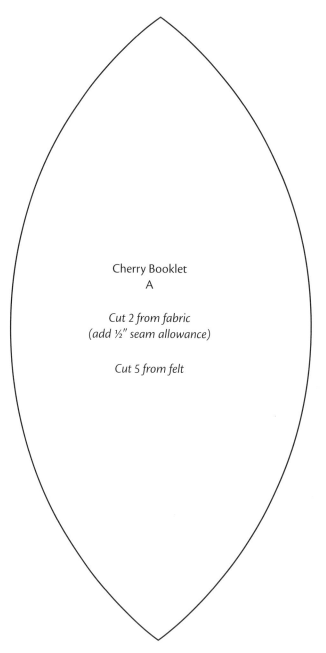

Cherry Booklet
A

*Cut 2 from fabric
(add ½" seam allowance)*

Cut 5 from felt

Miniature Kimono *see pages 112–117*

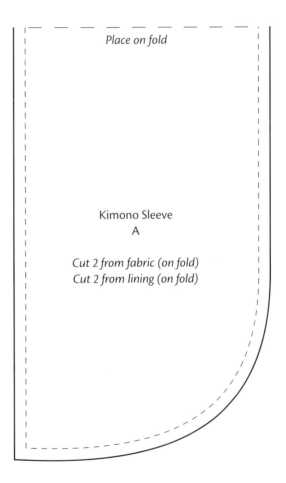

Place on fold

Kimono Sleeve
A

Cut 2 from fabric (on fold)
Cut 2 from lining (on fold)

Fishie Pouch see pages 120 123

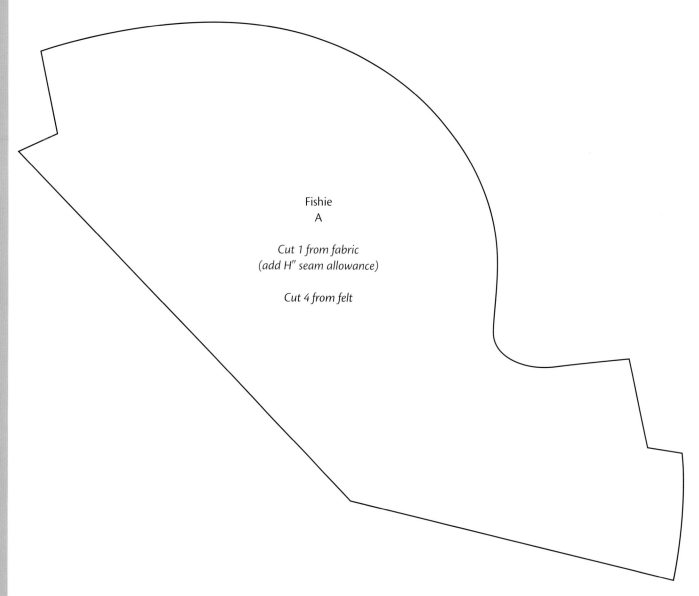

Fishie
A

Cut 1 from fabric
(add H" seam allowance)

Cut 4 from felt

Fishie Pouch *see pages 120–123*

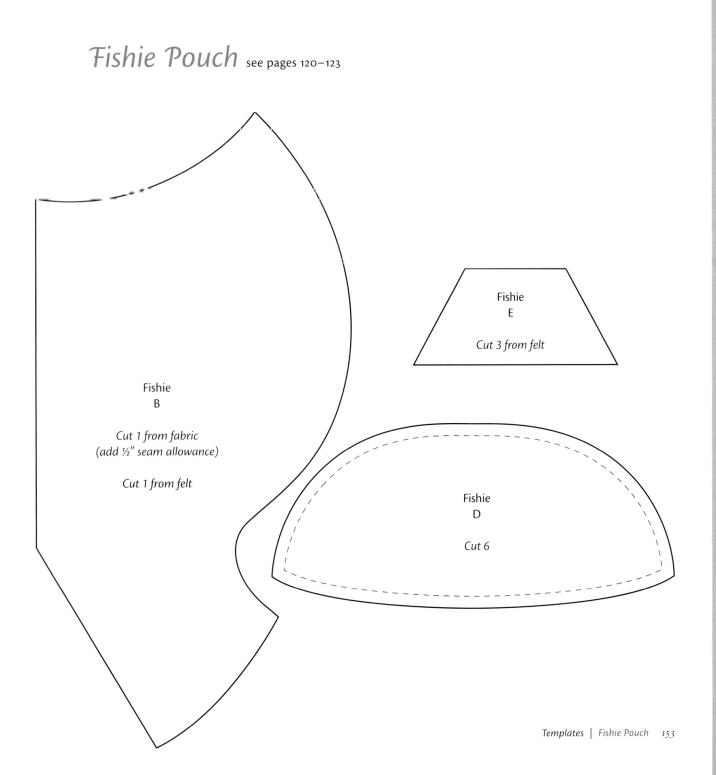

Fishie
E

Cut 3 from felt

Fishie
B

*Cut 1 from fabric
(add ½" seam allowance)*

Cut 1 from felt

Fishie
D

Cut 6

Dragonofly Cache see pages 124–127

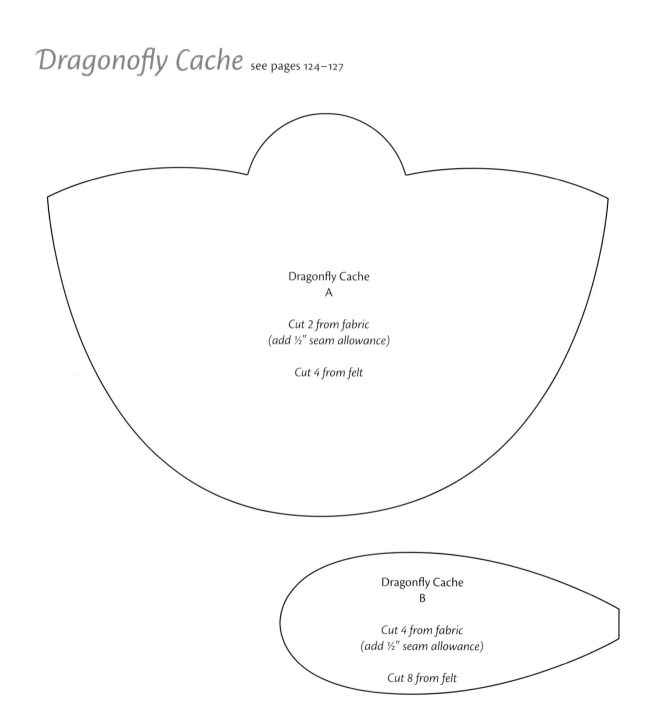

Dragonfly Cache
A

Cut 2 from fabric
(add ½" seam allowance)

Cut 4 from felt

Dragonfly Cache
B

Cut 4 from fabric
(add ½" seam allowance)

Cut 8 from felt

Aloha see pages 128–131

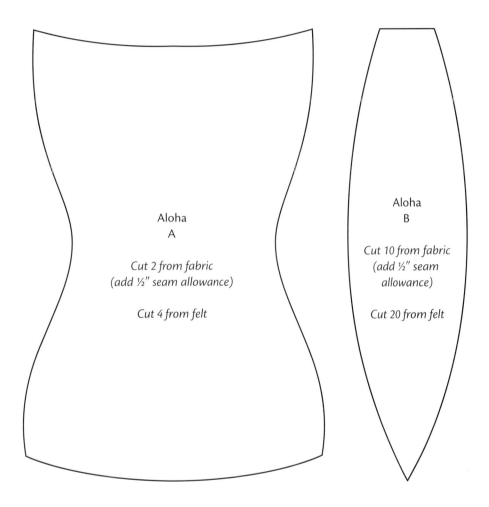

Aloha
A

Cut 2 from fabric
(add ½" seam allowance)

Cut 4 from felt

Aloha
B

Cut 10 from fabric
(add ½" seam
allowance)

Cut 20 from felt

Cicada see pages 132–135

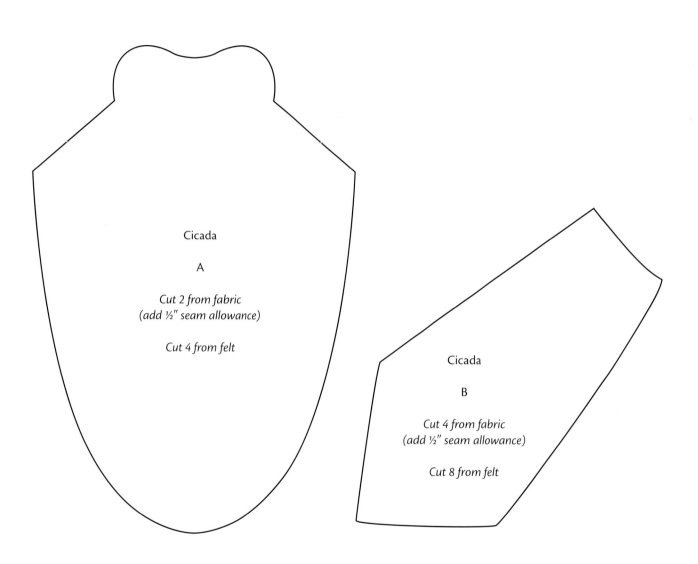

Cicada

A

Cut 2 from fabric
(add ½" seam allowance)

Cut 4 from felt

Cicada

B

Cut 4 from fabric
(add ½" seam allowance)

Cut 8 from felt